THE
LESS
PEOPLE
KNOW
ABOUT
US

THE LESS PEOPLE KNOW ABOUT US

A MYSTERY *of* BETRAYAL,
FAMILY SECRETS, *and* STOLEN IDENTITY

AXTON BETZ-HAMILTON

GRAND CENTRAL
PUBLISHING

NEW YORK   BOSTON

Grand Central Publishing / Hachette Book Group
1290 Avenue of the Americas, New York, NY 10104
grandcentralpublishing.com
twitter.com/grandcentralpub

First Edition: October 2019

Grand Central Publishing is a division of Hachette Book Group, Inc. The Grand Central Publishing name and logo is a trademark of Hachette Book Group, Inc.

The publisher is not responsible for websites (or their content) that are not owned by the publisher.

The Hachette Speakers Bureau provides a wide range of authors for speaking events. To find out more, go to www.hachettespeakersbureau.com or call (866) 376-6591.

Additional copyright acknowledgments are on page 307.

Library of Congress Cataloging-in-Publication Data
Names: Betz-Hamilton, Axton, author.
Title: The less people know about us : a mystery of betrayal, family secrets, and stolen identity / Axton Betz-Hamilton.
Description: First edition. | New York : Grand Central Publishing, [2019]
Identifiers: LCCN 2019011217| ISBN 9781538730287 (hardcover) |
ISBN 9781538730270 (ebook) | ISBN 9781549115165 (audio download)
Subjects: LCSH: Deception. | Secrecy. | Betrayal. | Identity theft.
Classification: LCC HV6691 .B473 2019 | DDC 364.16/33092--dc23
LC record available at https://lccn.loc.gov/2019011217

ISBNs: 978-1-5387-3028-7 (hardcover), 978-1-5387-3027-0 (ebook)

Printed in the United States of America

LSC-C

10 9 8 7 6 5 4 3 2 1

This book is dedicated to all identity theft victims. May you find the strength and courage to pursue your case until its closure, regardless of the time it takes.

PROLOGUE

It HAD BEEN A LONG DAY at school and the roots of a
headache had planted themselves near the outer corners of my
eyes. There were hours of homework in my immediate future
but as I walked through the parking lot of my building, I
wistfully considered a nap. The manila envelope I found folded
over and jammed in my mailbox was the last thing I wanted to
deal with.

With a groan of resignation, I yanked it from the box. It was
a lot bigger than I had expected a credit report to be. *Must come
with a lot of instructions*, I thought. Most of me wanted to drop it
by the front door and forget about it for a while, but I leaned
against the arm of my hand-me-down, green-floral-print couch
with my legs crossed and tore it open instead.

There have been a few moments in my life when reality has
skipped in front of me like a broken television—and I remember
this one in slow motion. Sliding my finger under the thick flap of
that envelope, feeling the adhesive give way and the paper tear
in jagged intervals—those were the last indelible sensations of
an existence I understood. And then, as sure as the sharp edges

of paper in my hands, another existence took its place. A new life, a different identity.

I did not find any instructions inside the envelope. Instead, I found the report, with the bulk of a term paper, full of fraudulent credit card charges and collection agency entries in my name. Discover, Bank One, First USA. Pages of numbers and dates as foreign as a language I did not speak. The first line of credit had been opened in 1993, when I was eleven. That was the year my parents' identities had been stolen.

My credit score was 380. For a merciful second I thought maybe that was good. After all, 100 is perfect. It always had been in school, anyway. Then I saw the corresponding key. My score of 380 placed me in the second percentile of all scorers in the United States. About as low as it gets.

As my body folded over the arm of the couch, my mind struggled to make sense of these bizarre numbers. *Surely they'll know—I was just a kid; I couldn't have done this.* I felt the sting of tears on my cheeks. *Who would do this to me?*

PART I

ONE

ALTHOUGH TODAY I QUESTION the legitimacy of my own claim, for many years I believed that Grandpa Elliott was the first resident of Jay County to own a satellite dish. I remember the colossal shadow it cast across the backyard, where it stood planted behind the limestone exterior of his single-story, ranch-style house. In the summers, heat would hover above its concave face, bending the fields behind it into a green vapor. On many afternoons when I was outside, helping Dad feed the animals, I would hear the growl of its motor, shifting the dish from one side of the Indiana sky to the other. Nesting deep in his brown La-Z-Boy, Grandpa had changed the channel.

I would follow its arc with my eyes as it inched from a White Sox game to the evening news. The cold automation of hard, beige metal moving against the blooming countryside: it almost didn't seem real.

My grandfather bought the satellite dish so that he could watch his games: the Pacers, the Hoosiers, the White Sox. It was a happy accident (for me) that it also delivered cartoons to the rural farmhouse. This new development provided a serious upgrade to the hours my grandfather and I spent together after school, before Mom came home from work. Ostensibly, *he* was supposed to be watching *me*, but I was the one who did most of the caretaking. Grandpa suffered from severe arthritis—among lots of other ailments—so I became a shuttle for the things he needed around the house: his pills, his drink, the remote. His fingers and wrists were so tangled in pain that I was his designated beer-opener. The *whissska* of the Old Milwaukee can and the tiny escaping bubbles that tickled my palm filled me with pride every time I popped one open.

I didn't mind doing those things for him. It made me feel important. That a towering man like my grandfather would let me take part in the sacred rituals of his life meant more to me than any 4-H ribbon ever would.

He had been in poor health for decades when he had the heart attack. More than the stomach ulcers or the poor circulation or the arthritis, though, Grandpa seemed to suffer most from an unrelenting awareness of his own mortality. He rarely left the house and when he did it was so that Sassy, his wool-white toy poodle, could enjoy a ride in the passenger seat. The decor strewn along the mantel had been gathering dust for decades. When he was diagnosed with depression, he washed his antidepressants down with a lunchtime shot of Canadian Club whiskey.

This grim outlook was how he convinced my parents to stay on the farm in the first place. They had moved a mobile home onto the land before I was born, relocating from Muncie back to Portland, and intending only to stay while my grandmother, Lelah, battled breast cancer. Like my parents, Grandpa wasn't actually expecting Lelah to die, and when she did, the impact was sharp. For months after, Grandpa remained morose and surly, moaning incessantly about what would become of him, what would become of the farm. His despondency wore on my mother's conscience. She agreed to stay nearby for a while, but reiterated that eventually she and my dad would need to move on to a place with the kind of social opportunities she craved, a place where she could make some real money. Dad felt confident about a job transfer to Bloomington, and Mom often looked forward aloud to their new life in Brown County, a picturesque slice of the state that lured visitors with its rolling hills and startling foliage.

But, somehow, there they were, all those years later, in the small town they had both grown up in. My dad had essentially become a full-fledged hobby farmer and the only home I had ever known was this farm, where just a driveway separated us from Grandpa. Fifteen years after she witnessed her mother succumb to cancer, Mom prepared to watch her father slip away.

It was a Saturday in March when the blood suddenly stopped flowing to my grandfather's heart, triggering massive kidney failure. He was rushed to the hospital, where doctors stabilized him but informed my parents the end was near. My grandfather seemed to will himself better then, or at least better enough to be released so that he could die at home. Against my father's wishes (ever practical, my father thought it an appropriate time for hospice), but with my mother's blessing, Grandpa returned to the limestone farmhouse. He was perched in the living room one day when I came in from school. Mute with pain, he leaned back against the rented medical recliner and stared at the ceiling like he was trying to think of a word he had forgotten. My eleven-year-old body recoiled in fear of his unrecognizable form.

For the next few days, my parents assigned me to rounds of supervision when they couldn't be in the house. Midweek, I was instructed to sit with Grandpa while Mom worked and

Dad tended the farm. By now, Grandpa was stationed in the back bedroom, the one that would become mine, in a rented hospital bed. Mom had dressed him in a red sweat suit; the activewear wilted on his dying body. I read a book aloud to fill the silence.

"I'm hot," he suddenly said, interrupting my dutiful recitation, tugging at his sweatshirt. I put my book down slowly and glanced through the door in the direction of the living room. There was no backup in sight.

"Grandpa, I know. But just leave that on, okay?" I knew that just as soon as he would take it off he'd be too cold, clutching for the balled-up comforter at his feet.

"I'm too damn hot!" he said louder, this time yanking the bottom edge of his sweatshirt up to his chin, his pale, skinny belly exposed.

"Grandpa, please don't. Mom and Dad said—" I stood up and put my hands near his chest, but I didn't know quite where to place them. It seemed wrong to work against the last gusts of his energy. I watched as his ragged face emerged from the inside-out ribs of the crewneck.

"Axton! Why did you let him take off his shirt?" Dad was suddenly behind me.

"I tried to stop him! He said he was hot!" I said, hands up in defense.

"George, I know you're hot." My dad's voice was void of patience. He pushed past me gently, picked up the damp sweatshirt, and began to fold it. "You hungry? The doctor said you can have anything you want. What'll it be?"

"Sherbet and Old Milwaukee" was my grandfather's immediate answer.

Without a word, I walked to the kitchen to grab a beer.

* * *

Grandpa slipped into a coma two days later. On Saturday, Mom was home from work, marching in and out of the back bedroom like a palace guard, every fifteen minutes on the dot. I had been outside with Dad feeding the animals, but came in to get a Coke from Grandpa's harvest-gold side-by-side refrigerator. Suddenly my mom screamed from the back bedroom.

"Axton! Get your dad! Grandpa's not breathing!"

My feet were already moving when I processed what Mom was saying. I shoved shoulder-first through the brown storm door and into the fading afternoon toward the barn. Dad wasn't far; one loud bellow was all it took.

Back inside, I arranged myself on the orange, flower-print La-Z-Boy like a doll on a shelf, my back straight and my hands on my knees. The moment felt enormous. I didn't have to strain to hear Dad consoling Mom, who was making noises I'd never heard her make.

They emerged from the back bedroom together, my father's arms around Mom's shoulders as he led her slowly into the living room. Her face was shiny with tears and her chest was jerking in sharp and sudden heaves.

"He's gone," my dad said to me, placing Mom onto the couch.

"Go say goodbye, Axton," Mom said between sobs.

As I stood up, my parents didn't move; I realized they wanted me to go in there alone. I walked down the short hall, my breath evading me. I didn't want to cry in front of my grandfather—he was always so analytical, so convinced that everything could be handled with reason—but I couldn't help it. There was only one overhead light shining in his bedroom, and below it, Grandpa looked fast asleep.

I stood next to his bed for a while. I studied the trophy he kept on his dresser: a miniature golden boy frozen in mid-layup above the words *Portland High School, Sectional Champions, 1926.* Grandpa had been a sophomore on the team. He went on to play in college, before the Depression cost him his basketball scholarship.

"I'm gonna do so much with my life, Grandpa," I said, suddenly full-on sobbing. "I'm gonna try out for the sixth-grade basketball team, I promise."

I don't remember what else I said or tried to say, only that I wished he would wake up and ask me to pass the remote. Soon, the funeral home would arrive and wheel my grandfather past us in a thick, black body bag, just like in the movies.

My mother was inconsolable.

* * *

"Wear the dress, Axton!"

"Mom! It's so ugly! I'm not wearing it."

"Axton, you will wear the dress!"

This dispute had been going on for nearly an hour. Dad had long since excused himself to find something to do out in the barn.

"Greg and Kathy spent good money on that dress, and you're going to wear it."

"Grandpa would have wanted me to be comfortable," I howled, absolutely convinced that it was true. Grandpa was a terrible dresser, regularly mixing plaids and stripes. He didn't care. He knew what really mattered.

I had worn the dress, a light blue floral number with a white collar to match the white faux-leather shoes it came with, to my baptism just a week prior. Greg and Kathy, my mom and dad's friends who were now my godparents, gifted it to me for the event. I liked Greg and Kathy—they owned the skating rink in Winchester where I spent most of my free time—but in my mind, my baptism was to be the first and the last time I donned that awful thing. The pattern looked like an old couch and the shoes squeaked like dog toys when I walked.

"Everyone is going to be there this afternoon," she retorted. "They expect you to look good." In the days since Grandpa died, Mom's few soft edges had sharpened. She seemed only to be either crying or yelling. With her father gone, she was a child without supervision. It was like her rope to harbor had snapped, and now she was adrift and flailing.

In the end, I wore a white dress shirt and black plaid slacks to Grandpa's funeral. I'm not sure I looked pretty like Mom wanted but I felt more like myself. When we arrived at the funeral home, I fought my way through a jungle of pantyhose and polyester suit legs to find my friend from the skating rink, Carrie. Together we explored the alcoves of the funeral home, eventually roosting in the powder room. We sat on the pink padded stools, under the bright glow of the vanity lights, looking at each other in the mirror. We talked about school and the skating rink. I appreciated that Carrie didn't ask me anything about Grandpa, about his body or how he died in what was going to be my new bedroom.

Suddenly, the echoes of my mother's laughter enveloped us. Her cackling seemed to bounce from wall to wall, rising well above the steady din of the crowd. I looked with wide eyes at Carrie, who was already looking at me. We wordlessly slid off our stools and crept down the hallway to see what was so hysterical.

I zeroed in on her, standing in the front of the room with an old friend. Like a street performer, she moved her arms in exaggerated gestures and maintained an unnaturally large smile. Every few beats she threw her head back and unleashed another terrible guffaw.

Directly behind her, my grandfather lay in his casket, his face rose-touched and rubbery.

"What do you think is wrong with my mom?" I asked Carrie.

Carrie offered a sincere shrug.

Whatever was wrong with my mom continued throughout the day, after the service and back at the house, where we hosted everyone for dinner. She didn't return to her normal self until the last guest had left, late in the evening. Then she slid out of her heels and onto the couch, where she would stay for the next six months.

Out in the yard, the satellite dish turned and searched the empty night sky for the Home Shopping Network.

TWO

I GREW UP IN JAY COUNTY, Indiana, on the flat eastern edge of the state, a place where livestock easily outnumber people, and time is measured in crop cycles and church calendars. There isn't a lot of money in Jay County, and most folks there lived modestly, including us. My grandfather's one-hundred-acre farm was by far the most valuable asset in the family. It sat seven miles south of the city of Portland, a small enclave of about six thousand people, with a low-slung courthouse and town square, where we would go to the post office and get books from the library, where we would pick up a bucket of Lee's Famous Recipe Chicken for special family dinners.

Family dinners were actually a rare event for us. Mom was never a cook, Dad was so busy, and neither was particularly close with their siblings. But sometimes, Grandpa would give Mom a twenty-dollar bill and instruct her to go get us some fried chicken. He didn't have to explain anymore that "a bucket of fried chicken" also meant fries from McDonald's and, since Mom was already there, a hamburger for Sassy the poodle. McDonald's hamburgers were Sassy's favorite. Then we'd gather around Grandpa's table for our greasy feast, eating our chicken off old yellow plates stamped with red roosters.

Other nights Dad and I would forage in the garden, choosing a random assortment of ripe vegetables and bringing them back to our small kitchen in the mobile home. I would wash our haul and Dad would do the chopping. Without prejudice, we'd mix everything together in one large pot with butter, pepper, salt, and garlic. I thought this method of preparation was quite fun; Mom thought it was gross. She never joined us for our one-pot meals.

But Mom was like that. She didn't go in for the farm stuff. She had, after all, never meant to come back here, to this land where she grew up, her bedroom window facing the same ash tree she used to play beneath. In a way, she had been an only child like me. Her half brothers were well into their teenage years when she was born, so she had grown up enjoying the undivided attention of her parents, and, when it behooved her, their inattention, too. By the time I was born, Uncles Mike and Larry didn't come around much anymore, except on Christmas and Easter. Grandpa Elliott had been the only father they'd ever known, but once their mother died, the already loose family bond seemed to slacken even more.

Back then, I was too preoccupied with my 4-H projects to lament my lack of cousins. I was also studying the anatomy of farm animals for my first 4-H competition. I had been waiting to join 4-H, the nationwide youth program that encourages agriculture-based service learning, practically my whole life, it seemed, or at least as long as I had been going to the county fair.

Watching the older kids with their goats and chickens stirred something deep within me. Dad had been in FFA, and when I turned ten—at last eligible for 4-H—he helped me acquire bantam chickens (known as miniature chickens to anyone not brought up on a farm) to raise and show at my first 4-H fair. The months of feeding, caring for, and getting to know my chickens were as exciting as I had always known they would be. I felt completely at home in the barn. I still do.

And yet, anxiety sat like heavy stones in my belly on the way to the fair. Looking over at me sympathetically from the driver's side, Dad tried to ease my nerves.

"Don't expect to win," he instructed. "This is just your first year. This is just practice. You're here to learn."

I nodded. But I wasn't nervous about winning or losing, simply getting through it. What if the judges asked me questions I didn't know the answers to? What if my rooster got spooked and flopped me? What if I tripped in front of everybody?

With my expectations so low, I was at a loss when, hours later, a judge placed the junior showmanship trophy on top of my rooster's cage. Befuddled, I turned to my father, who stood just behind me.

"Does he mean me?" I asked, pointing to myself. My father smiled proudly and nodded yes. It was the best day of my young life.

Except for one thing. Grandpa wasn't there. Lacking the stamina to stand in the poultry barn for hours at time, he had wished me luck that morning from his recliner. I couldn't wait to get home and wow him with my trophies and the slew of ribbons I ended up winning for my chickens. When we passed his truck going the other way on our ride home, I was deflated. He and Sassy were making their daily trip into town and I'd have to wait awhile to show him my winnings. But Dad had a plan.

"Why don't we go into the house and spread out all your ribbons and trophies on the table?" he said with a coy smile.

So we snuck into Grandpa's house and turned his kitchen into my personal trophy case. When he walked in through the garage door an hour later, Sassy under his arm, I was there waiting. He froze in the doorway. A rare smile bloomed across his face.

"Well? Tell me *all* about it!" Grandpa said, as if he wasn't even surprised at all.

Mom was happy for me, too, but she didn't wholly approve of 4-H. She said it was "full of cheats and liars" after a controversy involving a sheep and some ice cubes a couple of years back. Small-town life was like that—gossip and grudges—but I for one wasn't going to let it get in the way of something I was good at. As the only kid at home, and not exactly a social butterfly at school, 4-H made me feel as if I was a part of something, and I liked that.

In so many ways, I was luckier than a lot of the kids in Jay County, who waited for the bus in front of ramshackle, run-down houses. But I felt different from them, too, like my family didn't quite belong. Maybe it was because we didn't have big Sunday dinners, as was so common among my class-mates. Maybe it was because our family was fragmented, its history, I was learning, brimming with divorces and abusive relationships. Or that we didn't technically belong to a church until my mother decided she wanted me baptized. Maybe it was because my mom refused to act like everybody else's, that after one year of being a homeroom mother, she wasn't invited back. Whatever it was that set us apart, I felt it even more intensely after Grandpa died. And when Mom got depressed, our already unconventional system—unmoored from the pillars that seemed to stabilize all the other families around us—seemed precariously close to collapse.

THREE

I KEPT WAITING FOR THINGS to go back to the way they were. I kept waiting for a bucket-of-chicken night or an afternoon at the skating rink. As we slowly transferred our things from the mobile home to Grandpa's house, I yearned for a sign that, at some point, we would be us again.

But every afternoon when I came in the front door, still wearing my backpack, I would find her there, zoned out in front of the TV on Grandpa's old Halloween-colored couch. Usually the phone had been moved from the yellow Formica bar that separated the living room and kitchen to the seat next to Mom. Sometimes she would be on it when I came inside. As I spread out my homework on the floor of my new bedroom, my 4-H ribbons tacked up across the walls, I would listen to her politely request the color earrings she wanted, the length of the necklace.

She called it "cheap, chunky jewelry." It was chunky—shiny and hollow like Christmas tree ornaments—but I wasn't sure how cheap it could be considering how much of it she bought. When we did leave the house for church or to shop, she would show it off to her friends. "Look at my new ring," she would say, momentarily reanimated by someone's attention. In those moments, I always felt surprised to learn that the purpose of these flashy things was not for her to look good but to be looked *at*.

No one ever taught me to worry about money, but I did anyway, and from a very early age. My parents deliberated often and openly about what and what not to spend money on, and they spoke in hushed tones about their financial anxieties—the normal, middle-class calculus of getting by—when they thought I couldn't hear. It seemed obvious that we were better off than most of the kids I went to school with, but in Jay County, that didn't mean much. And I knew for sure that we didn't have the kind of money for all that pointless jewelry.

Those afternoons stretched on across seasons. Summer turned to autumn, and Mom was still making calls, reciting our address and credit card number like multiplication tables. She started sending me across the busy highway we lived on to retrieve the packages, and recruited me to help clean up the wrapping a few minutes before Dad was due home from his shift at the grocery. Only then would she get off the couch to make herself busy elsewhere, returning the phone to its position on the counter.

"I don't think you should buy any more jewelry, Mom," I told her one afternoon, finding my courage.

"Oh, Axton. It's just chintzy stuff. It's not hurting anyone," she said dismissively, lit up by the glow of the TV.

A few days later, I found another package stuffed in the mailbox. When I delivered it to Mom on the couch, she stiffened with glee, insisting that I open this one. Inside, there were two identical gold rings, a roaring lion balanced on each. The lions' heads were studded with little fake rubies. They looked like bedazzled door knockers. One was for me, she said, and watched with a smile as I pushed the cat by his ears down my skinny finger.

I was glad to see her happy, but my complicity in her new hobby didn't make me feel special the way fetching Grandpa's beer had.

* * *

My mother was in business for herself back then. She worked as a tax and payroll preparer for people and local businesses in the area. Prior to that she had been working for an insurance office when her boss told her that she was savvy enough and ought to start her own business. Mom was never one to ignore a compliment.

Mom at work at Porter-Takats, an insurance office, sometime in the mid-'80s.

Capitalizing on the contacts she had made at the insurance office, my mother was successful in attracting a moderate amount of business. Sometimes she would let me ride with her as she made the rounds to pick up paperwork from her clients. My favorite of these trips was to Jinny's Café, a truck stop in the tiny town of Bryant. My great-grandmother had worked at Jinny's—before it was called that—when US 27 was the main route from Florida to Michigan. It remained a small restaurant with a few gas pumps out front for cars and a couple more on the side for long-haulers. Mom made me wait in the truck, and while she went inside to collect time sheets and gossip, I would imagine what the place looked like when Grandma's mother showed up for her shift. In my mind the scene was in black and white, my great-grandmother smoothing out her apron.

After Grandpa died, there were fewer of these excursions. Mom was clearly getting her work done somehow, but she seemed to have lost her entrepreneurial spark. Some field trips did continue, though. I looked forward to our monthly outings to the mall. It meant a stop at the bookstore but also an escape from the dark living room of the house.

What eventually became our special mother-daughter dates had begun as a part of the elaborate choreography of Grandpa's medical routine. Every Wednesday near the end of his life, my mother would drive her dad to Dayton for chelation therapy to treat his poor circulation. While he was hooked up to the machines all afternoon, the heavy metals being sucked from his bloodstream, Mom would venture to the Salem Mall. Eventually, she started to let me skip school on Wednesdays so she would have a shopping companion. Back at the outpatient center, we'd reclaim Grandpa, fatigued and plagued by the smell of garlic, an unfortunate side effect of his treatment.

These day-trips turned into such a routine that my teachers began to question the real reason behind my absences. I defiantly told them they could ask my mother about it.

I was relieved when Mom still showed interest in the hour drive to the mall despite losing a member of our traveling party—not to mention our excuse for going. Once a month, now on Saturdays, we adhered to the same routine. First, the bookstore for me, where I would find the latest installment of *The Baby-Sitters Club* or the *Sweet Valley High* series. Afterward, we would visit Mom's favorite store, Added Dimensions. It sold plus-sized clothes, but the kind Mom liked, the kind, as she put it, that weren't "Walmart-y." I would sit on the bench outside the store and devour my new novel while she tried on blouses and more jewelry. Our last stop was usually to the drugstore, where Mom would encourage me to choose new nail polish. I still wasn't allowed to wear makeup but Mom liked it when I painted my fingernails a pale pink.

Sometimes on the way home we would stop at Maid-Rite, a famous loose meat sandwich joint in western Ohio. The wall of the tiny restaurant was covered in people's discarded gum, and rumor had it the meat was marinated in Mountain Dew.

This ritual, these small treats made me feel special; I liked Mom paying attention to me and including me in the things that brought her joy. But I knew that while she had a lot of clients, most of them were small businesses that paid her Portland, Indiana, rates. My parents had always been responsibly austere, and I wasn't sure where all this money was coming from.

Anyway, for me, the best part about the long days with Mom had nothing to do with buying things. My favorite moments were the drives back and forth from Portland. As we sailed along two-lane roads, through the low fields of the countryside, we would fill the cab of her GMC truck with talk about school and the animals, which girls in my class I was close with—it was never very many. My mother gave me what felt like insider advice on which cliques to avoid (as if I had a choice in the matter) and whose parents were unpleasant—she knew them from her own days at East Jay Junior High. She'd tell me secrets about Dad's family and regale me with stories of her own. These admissions and admonishments solidified in my head as undisputed truth. My mother's word was gospel.

Once, several months after Grandpa Elliott died, she took me to see her mother's friend Ruth in a suburb close to Dayton, Ohio. Mom wanted me to have some connection to my grandmother, she said, some way of knowing about the life and the version of Grandma Elliott I would never encounter firsthand. We sat in the old woman's living room for most of the afternoon, as I chided myself to pay attention through hours of storytelling.

Even at that age, I sensed the depth of my mother's longing for her dead parents and the past they shared. She reminisced lovingly about the family's mobile home on Indian Lake, a popular vacation spot across the Ohio state line. She confided that she had been trying to sway Dad to buy a home there for years but he wouldn't consider it. He said we couldn't afford it and that he hated Indian Lake anyway. I couldn't understand how anyone wouldn't want to live in the magical place Mom remembered, and thought maybe we should save up our jewelry money and convince Dad it was possible. I thought that maybe if we lived at Indian Lake, Mom would get off the couch more, invite her brothers over for holiday dinners again.

As it was, these trips to Dayton were the only time I could

pry her eyes from the TV. On the Mondays after our weekend trips I would come home from school hopeful she was feeling better. But when I'd open the door, the first thing I'd see was the empty place on the Formica counter where the phone should have been.

FOUR

My mother wasn't one to dwell on or even talk about her dreams. As a family, our conversations about dreams began and ended with recounting only the truly bizarre, usually for a laugh. So when she began describing the haunting and recurring nighttime visions she started having almost a year after Grandpa's death, Dad and I were worried.

She said that in the dream she was at Indian Lake—the Indian Lake of her childhood—frantically searching for her parents. They needed her. She could hear their voices. But no matter how many nights the dream came, it always ended the same way: her search was futile.

At the same time that these dreams began, Mom was seeing her OB-GYN often, seeking treatment for hormone-related weight issues and what she was beginning to realize—and what I was able to piece together from overheard conversations—was situational depression that resulted from her father's death. After one of these appointments, she came home and announced that she needed to make a pilgrimage to Indian Lake—doctor's orders. Perhaps, the doctor said, Mom could replace the old

Indian Lake in her head with the new one, the one where her parents had died and time had moved on.

I was elated when Mom asked me to join her. I knew the day would be a solemn occasion but it would also be my chance to finally experience the magic I'd gleaned only from her stories. On the Saturday morning we left, it was all I could do to suppress my bubbling excitement beneath a serious face. I didn't want Mom to think I wasn't taking her distress seriously.

It took about an hour and a half to get to the lake, and on the way, Mom told me stories I had heard dozens of times, about her weekends there with Grandma, the haunted roller rink, the Sandy Beach Amusement Park. I loved them all. Mom's childhood seemed so exciting compared to mine, so exotic.

The road we traveled that day had carried my mother and her own mother from Portland to Indian Lake countless times, so that they could trade the Indiana cornfields for lakeside cocktails. Grandma Elliott was from Ohio, and had moved to Jay County to find work in the glass factories that dotted north central Indiana. The Indiana gas belt—at the turn of the century the largest deposit of natural gas ever discovered—had triggered a full-on industrial revolution in our corner of the state. The gas fields were so massive that when coal miners first stumbled upon them, the terrifying roar of escaping pressure was enough to convince the men that they had punctured the ceiling of hell. This vast reserve of fuel enticed a slew of burgeoning companies—Ball and U.S. Steel among them—to build factories in the area. At one point in its history, the tiny town of Dunkirk had one thousand residents and twenty-three glass factories. It was known as the Glass Capital of Indiana.

The little I know about my grandmother's life unspools like a soap opera. She was married at sixteen. She had two children,

Mom and Grandma Elliott, 1960.

my uncles Mike and Larry, with her first husband, who was by all accounts an alcoholic. Family lore says that Grandma, too, had a dangerous proclivity for drinking in her youth. Just a few years into their young marriage, Lelah's husband beat her severely, causing her to miscarry their third child. A devout Catholic, she sought—and received—her priest's blessing to get a divorce. According to Mom, Grandma went on a wild streak then. Still a teenager, she left the boys at an orphanage and ran off to California. After a stalled modeling career and two more failed marriages, she came back to Dunkirk, where she found work in a bar—my grandpa Elliott's. Even when I was young I could imagine why my grandfather was drawn to Grandma, the lovely but hard-boiled barmaid in his saloon. Lelah cast a spell on my grandfather. She was twenty-nine when they married. It was his first wedding; it was her fourth. After their wedding, according to Mom, Grandpa Elliott directed Grandma Elliott to go to Fort Wayne and get her sons, who by that time were living with their uncle Smoke and aunt Grace.

George worked hard to provide for Grandma and her boys, and soon my mother, too, who was born not long after the nuptials. Eventually, Grandma became my grandfather's business partner, providing secretarial support for the growing alcohol distribution company he had inherited from his sister and brother-in-law. They worked hard, and the stories indicate my grandmother especially enjoyed the fruits of their labor. There were rumors of affairs, and Grandpa once admitted to dragging Grandma out of another man's house not long after Mom came along. Unlike the others, though, this marriage stuck. Grandpa provided her with the life—and the freedom—she had wanted all along.

"Have I ever told you about that time Grandpa fell into the lake?" my mom asked, turning the radio low. Outside, the fields were smudged with the smallest hints of green and my winter jacket was slung around my waist.

"No—tell me!" I said. I knew the story by heart.

"Well, they were all partying on the dock, drinking, having a good time." In Mom's stories about Indian Lake, people were always partying, and no one ever had anything but a good time. "And Grandpa was telling a story, not paying attention to where his feet were—and ended up falling off the dock and into the lake!" she said with a snort.

Mike, Larry, and my mother, sometime in the 1960s.

I laughed with her, though the thought made me a little sad. I imagined my grandfather, in his polo shirt and knee-high socks, tumbling into dark water.

"And do you know what your grandmother shouted?" She looked over at me with wide grin.

I shook my head no.

"She said, 'Get his wallet! Get his wallet!'" Mom turned her eyes back to the road and sighed wistfully.

The story was in line with what I knew about my grandmother. Even in black-and-white photos, her jewelry glistened like candlelight, her long neck adorned in diamonds. These totems of wealth were a bluff, but Grandpa seemed to know how

Grandpa and Grandma Elliott.

to keep his wife happy. So that Grandma could get away, relax, and socialize, he bought a vacation mobile home for her to put on Indian Lake. She was thrilled. He had the pink-and-gray home towed to the place she had chosen—on a street called Fun Drive, on a sliver of land called Fantasy Island.

* * *

An unlikely vacation oasis among an expanse of farm plains, Indian Lake is a quiet place today. But in its heyday—during my grandmother's life and my mother's childhood—Indian Lake buzzed with activity. The Sandy Beach Amusement Park brought the boardwalk to the landlocked Ohio with roller coasters, a penny arcade, a Ferris wheel, and rowdy dance halls. One of the dance halls claimed to be the biggest and best in the Midwest, and routinely attracted world-class orchestras to town. Parades, boat shows, and fireworks filled the summer calendar.

The lore that surrounded the lake was even bigger than its fan-fare. Residents and tourists passed around rumors of Chicago mobsters lying low in lakeside cottages. Kids excitedly reported to one another that an abandoned mine was buried deep below the water. It was in this wonderland of secrets and glamour that my mother came of age.

The Indian Lake my mother had described was decidedly *not* the place we found that Saturday morning. Driving over the rickety bridge onto Fantasy Island, I could glimpse the rows of mobile homes, lined up close like schoolchildren, most of them too boxed in to see the water.

"Isn't this a fire hazard?" I asked before realizing I shouldn't.

"I guess so. No one really thought about things like that back then," she said, distracted. As if on autopilot, she steered the truck to the front of the small home that had been hers during her senior year of high school. She put the truck in park and I wondered if she was absorbing the scene, confirming that her parents were not here, that they did not still need her.

A teenager myself, I couldn't believe Mom had lived here on her own, not much older than I was now, and almost completely unsupervised. What I *really* couldn't believe was that my grand-parents had marooned my mom on this island to keep her away from Dad.

My father's aunt Patty introduced Mom and Dad when she was twelve and he was fourteen. Aunt Patty was a homecoming queen turned hairdresser, so she knew just about everyone in the county, including the Elliotts. Before they were even allowed to go on dates alone, Mom and Dad were a couple. My mom's parents tolerated Dad, though they introduced him to people at the Portland Country Club as "Pam's little farm boy." Dad always remembered that.

As my parents got older—and grew closer—Mom's folks worried she was hurtling toward marriage with little thought of a career or even an education. They told her they wouldn't pay for college or her car if she insisted on marrying Dad right after graduation. Obstinate and in love, my mother contended she was ready to be a wife. And so her parents sent her to Indian Lake, to give her a year without my father, and with that, hopefully, a chance to change her mind. Grandpa and Grandma continued working in Portland, and my grandmother drove to the mobile home every weekend to check in on my mom. Grandma left on Thursdays and returned on Sundays—each weekend in Indian Lake during Mom's senior year was a long weekend away from Portland for Grandma, which she loved.

"It was so fun here, Axton," Mom said, gazing at the mobile home. Gauzy curtains hung in the windows; this home was somebody else's now and I wondered if they could see us through them. "Really, though, it was the people who made it so great. Open-minded people. Not like in Portland."

I shifted in my seat to get a better view. This place didn't look that fun. The old roller coaster we had passed was buried in ivy, and broken glass glittered along Main Street. On the way into town, we drove by the diner where Mom had waited tables. A few abandoned letters remained on its sign; most of its paint was gone.

Despite being forced here against her will all those years ago, and despite the aging resort town it had become, Mom was relentless in her positive spin. Her senior year at Indian Lake High School turned out to be better than she could have imagined. She said the kids in Portland had been cruel, bullying and ostracizing her for being the daughter of sinful liquor peddlers. In Indian Lake she found a group of people who accepted and included her. That the legal drinking age in Ohio at the time was eighteen probably helped grease the wheels of my mother's blossoming.

It felt like we stayed there, idling and staring, for an hour. I wanted to tell her I was hungry, but feared I'd interrupt whatever important psychic mechanics might be going on in her head. When we did leave Fantasy Island, we drove by more landmarks from Mom's youth: after-school hangouts, so-and-so's house, the beach.

"Your grandparents found Dad here one night, waiting for me," she said, tapping the window as we drove by the marina. She smiled a sort of mischievous smile. "Grandpa was so angry, he called the police. Two cops showed up."

"What did Dad do?" I asked. This was a new story.

"He left town, stopped at the state line for a few minutes, and then turned around and came back," she said with a snicker.

"Did Grandpa find out?"

"Oh, eventually. They filed a restraining order against him." She turned the truck into the McDonald's parking lot.

"Who? Dad? They filed a restraining order against Dad?" I couldn't believe what I was hearing. I couldn't believe I was *just now* hearing it. I knew my grandparents disapproved of Dad, but not on a personal level. Sure, he was a poor farm kid, but his real sin in their eyes, I had always thought, was wanting to marry Mom too young.

"Yeah, against Dad," she confirmed, like it was some innocuous bit of family trivia. "Everybody got over it eventually."

It was late afternoon. We ordered burgers, fries, and Cokes from the drive-through and ate on our way back to Portland.

"You know," Mom said, interrupting our mealtime silence, "when your dad and I came back to the farm to take care of

Grandma, Grandpa took me out back—we were looking at the outbuildings and the fields—and he told me 'this will all be yours someday, Pam.'"

She let the words hang like fishing line; I felt like it was my turn to say something.

"Yeah?" I said, holding my half-eaten cheeseburger in both hands.

She shook her head. "But nobody even asked me if I wanted it."

We didn't say much else on the way back. Afternoon gave way to a dreary evening. We drove through the gas-boom towns—now as empty as a winter silo. In school I had learned that most of the gas had been wasted by these towns burning flambeaus—a flame to indicate the gas was on and flowing—day and night, for years on end. The light was purely symbolic, intended to demonstrate the economic vitality of the town to passersby. But it was an illusion, pure bluster. This superfluous show of strength quickly sucked all the gas from the ground and in a decade, the area's wealth and population withered again.

I put my forehead against the cool glass of the window. I counted cows lying down in their fields. I held my breath as we crossed the state line, getting ever farther from Fantasy Island, heading back to reality in Portland.

FIVE

By the time the daffodils bloomed that year, some semblance of normalcy—or at least a new kind of normalcy—was starting to take shape. Though she was still shopping too much, Mom had taken on a few new clients, and Dad had thrown himself headfirst into the farm, accumulating animals and planting acres upon acres of hay. He spent the first half of his day at the grocery, where he was the produce department manager, and the second half on the farm. If his fourteen-hour workdays exhausted him, he never let on.

For her birthday that year, Mom requested a day-trip to Whitewater Memorial State Park, one of her favorite places in Indiana, and Hueston Woods, a park just across the border in Ohio that we had visited often as a family. This was an impromptu decision, and one I was thrilled about. I put on my gym shoes and hoped my parents would let me walk around the nature center at Hueston Woods again. There was a rabbit there that when I was a toddler I had decided was *the* Easter Bunny. I still liked to go see it.

We rarely took extended vacations—the farm made that nearly

Dad, Mom, and me at Clifty Falls State Park on one of our rare weekend getaways.

impossible—but these day-trips around the state were happy occasions. Mom and Dad were always more affectionate when we were driving around some lake or down a leafy country road. Often I would notice them holding hands in the front seat. My mother especially came alive as Portland faded in the rearview.

Just as I was about to bound out of my room, the yelling started. I sat back down on my bed and listened. I couldn't believe Dad was acting like this on Mom's birthday. Since Grandpa died, it seemed my parents' rules of engagement had been upended. Occasional nervousness about money had turned into frequent and angry fights. Dad leveled an accusation that Mom was spending too much money and Mom wailed in objection. She needed more, she said, Dad didn't know how expensive things were. I sat on my bed and thought about the ruby-studded lion in my jewelry box. I thought about all the wrappings I had shoved down deep in the trash can like Mom had instructed. I closed my door gently.

A few hours later—after a tentative truce was reached—we were driving the scenic loop through Whitewater. A few fishermen in motor boats dotted the reservoir, and although the trees were still mostly bare, a verdant underbrush was beginning to transform the landscape into something more summery. From the backseat I could feel the tension between my parents as we sat in an icy silence. Mom's gaze was fixed beyond the guardrail and Dad gripped the wheel with both hands. When we got to Hueston Woods, I didn't ask to stop at the nature center. The only time we got out of the truck was to get gas. The few words my parents spoke pertained to directions.

The sun had set by the time we got back to the farm. Mom planted herself in front of the TV and Dad went out back to work on evening chores. I followed him into the barn. Before he even turned to acknowledge me, I blurted it out.

"She buys a lot of jewelry from the TV, Dad. And she shows it off. She told me not to tell you." The admission erupted from within me like a broken fire hydrant. My dad put his hands against the rough wall of the barn and exhaled in anger.

"And she makes me get it from the mailbox," I blurted.

My father snapped his head toward me and set his jaw hard. He was adamant I never cross the highway alone, and I understood why. It was busy. Sometimes our barn cats tried to follow me and I was afraid they would get hit by a car.

"You've been crossing the highway by yourself." He said it like a statement, not a question.

Part of me wished I could take it back. But a bigger part of me hoped that with the truth out in the open, my parents could resolve their ongoing arguments about money.

I was still visiting the animals in the barn when Dad

confronted Mom about what I had said. Whether it was a noisy crescendo or subdued surrender, I don't know. But soon after, the flow of cheap, chunky jewelry suddenly stopped for good.

* * *

It was during a previous trip to Hueston Woods that Dad had discovered a passion. I was still squirming in my car seat as he and Mom drove into the park. Posted near the entrance, my dad noticed a sign that said *Donkey Show* above a crooked arrow. His interest was piqued.

There are pictures from that afternoon. Whenever Mom got them out she loved to recount how curious my father was made by that sign. "What in the world could that be," he'd said. How he had driven the curving state park roads with his body hunched forward in his seat. When she got to the pictures of my father holding me, my arm reaching out to timidly pat one of the sturdy creatures, she remembers Dad saying, "I'm going to have one of these someday."

Ten years later, Dad and I were exploring the fall swap meet—an annual event where farmers sold and bought everything from old tractor parts to fuzzy baby chicks—at the Jay County Fairgrounds when we came upon a miniature donkey, docile in his small pen behind a handwritten sign that said *$300*. The donkey came home with us; his name was Odie.

While the rest of the farm resembled a modern-day Noah's Ark—a couple of llamas here, a duo of Bronze turkeys there—my father's commitment to raising donkeys endured, transitioning from miniature donkeys to mammoth donkeys. At the peak of his hobby farming, my dad had forty-seven donkeys. Donkeys, of course, have historically been used to carry heavy loads

Mom with the offspring of a donkey from our farm.

and protect sheep. My father's donkeys were for show and for trail riding.

A couple of weeks after Mom's birthday, I came in the back door and found my father in the kitchen, leaning against the counter with the receiver wedged between his shoulder and his head. He was studying the orange carpet with a furrowed brow. I took my time investigating the refrigerator.

"I'm not sure why I'm paying you if you're not going to send me anything," he said. I could hear his hand smack the counter with indignation. There was silence then, while someone somewhere explained something. So Dad wouldn't think I was eavesdropping, or get mad at me for leaving the fridge open too long, I returned to the backyard and my book.

At the table that night, where I was the only one eating some leftovers I had reheated myself, the mystery was revealed. My father's *The Brayer* magazine had not been arriving.

"Pam, I called them already," my father explained. "They

said they have absolutely been sent, and that it must be a problem on our end."

I moved the corn and squash around with my fork and thought about the last issue of the magazine I had seen on the end table. I guessed it *had* been a while. The magazines were more like monographs, each one thick and heavy like the JCPenney catalog. Sometimes when I was bored, I would attempt to read one of the articles—something about rescuing wild donkeys or breaking them for trail riding—but rarely made it through the first page before my curiosity waned.

My mother took a sip of her Diet Rite. "I think you should just cancel it," she said.

When the phone bills started disappearing, my mother showed more concern.

"It's definitely Willy," she announced one evening while we were watching TV in the living room. Dad was in his farm clothes, getting ready to go outside and feed the animals, and I was avoiding homework by lying on the carpet in front of the TV.

"That's a stretch, Pam," Dad said, incredulous.

"Think about it. Willy's son works at the phone company. I bet he's going down to the billing department and snatching ours out of the bunch."

My dad stood up, about to make his way to the barn. I flipped over on my elbows to see his reaction.

"Okay. If it's Willy, why is he taking my *Brayer* and *Mules and More*? That doesn't make a whole lot of sense."

"Yeah—and my pen pal letters, Mom? Why would anyone take those?" I interjected. No one seemed bothered that my friends' letters weren't arriving. As a twelve-year-old farm kid, those notes were my social lifeline. Since Greg and Kathy had sold the skating rink, I never saw Carrie anymore. She went to school in a different district and so we had taken to corresponding by mail. My Amish friend Katie also sent me letters during the summer.

My mother looked at me but I could tell my pen pal letters weren't high on her priority list.

"Obviously when we're all gone during the day, Willy, or someone over there, must be taking the mail." Mom stated her opinion as fact, as she always did.

My dad sighed and shook his head. "I'm going out to the barn. If you really think it's Willy, I'll go over there again," he said before disappearing into the dark kitchen and out the back door.

Willy lived on the parcel of land behind the farm. His place was so far back from the road, though, I had only ever seen him from a distance. I thought he was gaunt and mean-looking and felt his wife wore a permanent scowl.

Grandpa Elliott and Willy had waged a years-long war over two feet of land that Willy had thought was his. The land belonged to Grandpa—a surveyor came out to confirm that—but Grandpa said that Willy had at times moved segments of the fence line in the middle of the night. A few years before Grandpa died, Dad got fed up. With his rifle on the passenger seat, he kicked up plumes of dust as he sped down the gravel road to Willy's. Mom stationed herself in their bedroom, at the back of the mobile home, with the phone in her lap, listening hard for gunshots and ready to call the sheriff when she heard them. I sat next to her, my heartbeat loud in my ears.

We hadn't had trouble with Willy since then, but now

Mom's theory made sense. Our yellow metal mailbox stood unattended all day; Willy would have ample time to take what he wanted. It didn't seem likely he would steal our letters and magazines, but maybe he was just that mad about the property dispute.

Mom didn't send Dad over to Willy's. Instead, she got us a PO Box in Portland. She checked it every day on her way to or from a client's. Magazines, bills, and letters from Carrie and Katie still went missing.

One night, while Dad cut up vegetables from the garden, I listened from the living room as Mom explained that there were probably people working in the post office who were stealing our mail. Dad, skeptical, asked why anyone would do that.

"People steal your mail to get your social security number or your account information," she said with unearned authority. She had seen something on the news about something similar happening in the Muncie post office. I didn't hear Dad ask any more questions, just the rhythmic sound of his butcher's knife on the cutting board. A few days later, our phone was shut off.

* * *

"What am I supposed to do if something happens while I'm home alone? What if there's a fire?" Mom and I were making our monthly pilgrimage to the mall. I was trying to make the case that it wasn't safe for me to be home alone in the summer, without a working phone.

"Get the animals out, get yourself out, and let the place burn," she said dryly, not taking her eyes from the road.

I knew Mom was frustrated. She said she had spent hours

that week at the post office and police department begging for formal investigations to be launched. In the meantime, she had secured another PO Box in Albany, two towns over, in an attempt to stay in front of whoever was stealing our mail. At some point, Mom had begun calling what was happening to us identity theft.

Dad stayed out of Mom's way while she handled the crisis, diverting his attention to the farm. In high summer he was always buried in chores, sometimes taking a day off from the grocery just to bale hay. His equipment purchases hadn't quite kept pace with his ambition; the model 750 John Deere he had bought new in 1985 was woefully inadequate to handle the forty acres of hay he had planted in three years' time.

"Who do they think it is?" I reticently asked.

"They don't know, honey," she said, looking over her shoulder to merge onto I-70. "Probably somebody who doesn't like us."

The hair on my arms tingled. Who didn't like us? I couldn't think of one mean thing we'd done to anyone. What was it about us? Why were we good targets?

Several weeks later there was a break in the case. Mom came home with a cardboard box full of magazines and bills. She said the police had found it in an alley behind someone's house in Portland. Relieved, I excitedly pulled my pen pal letters from the pile atop the kitchen table. I was on my way to my room when I heard Dad raise his voice.

"Pam, this has gone too far. I'm going down there tomorrow to talk to them myself."

"You can't do that because you didn't file the police report— I did—so they can't talk to you about it," my mother said in exasperation.

I quietly shut my bedroom door. It didn't bother me that Mom and Dad were fighting; this whole thing would be taken care of soon, I thought.

I look back with a lot of pity on my twelve-year-old self. If only she knew how bad it was about to get.

SIX

THINGS DIDN'T GET BETTER. If they were even trying, the police seemed no closer to figuring out who was stealing our mail, and Mom and Dad's fighting had only gotten worse. Sometimes I thought it was a blessing the phone got shut off—one fewer bill for them to argue about. But as August loomed, I worried less about their troubles and more about my own. Eighth grade was approaching like a herd of vicious animals. The idea of walking back into East Jay Junior High turned my stomach to macramé. During the last week of school, I had been pushed down the stairs during passing period.

I was a bully's dream. I had chopped-off hair and glasses, read well above my grade level, and lacked an older sibling for protection. I was inept at sports. My parents didn't socialize with other parents, at least not ones from Jay County. The name-calling I could handle, but the physical torment pushed me to my breaking point. Once, a kid named Jason pulled my seat out from under me in front of everyone. I'll never forget the echoes of laughter as my back met the unforgiving vinyl tile below. A girl named Elizabeth used to sit on my lap, trying to force me to kiss her to prove to everyone I was a lesbian, as her and her disciples of friends liked to allege.

But it wasn't just the bullying—I was used to that. It was the boredom, the soul-crushing tedium of classes that felt so far below my capacity that we might as well have been smudging paint around with our fingers. I was old enough to know that private school would be better, and smart enough to know that private school was prohibitively expensive. As my parents continued to struggle to pay the bills, asking for anything extra felt profane. But self-preservation can be a powerful thing.

I remember it was a steamy morning, one of those mornings when it's hot before there's a sun to blame it on. I heard Mom in the family room, readying papers to take to a client. Dad had been gone for hours. I put on a shirt she liked me in, a green knit with a crew neck; Mom always liked what she called "nice knit tops." I filled a glass of water from the tap and looked over my shoulder. Mom was reaching for her purse.

"Mom, can I talk to you about something?"

"Yep." She was searching her bag for her keys. I couldn't tell if the note of frustration in her voice was about them or me.

"I don't want to go back to East Jay."

This got her attention. "Axton, we've talked about this."

"I hate it there. The kids are so mean. And bad. They behave like monsters. And the classes are so easy, Mom, I can do the homework in my sleep."

I knew I was speaking to a stacked audience. Mom looked at me sympathetically. Light from the front door infiltrated her bobbed, dark hair. She had started dyeing it that year to cover the gray that had been making its debut in conspicuous patches. She had gained more weight recently, despite her constant dieting.

"They call me a boy, Mom." I put my glass down to point at my head with both index fingers. "Because of my short hair. They say I'm *butch*. They call me a lesbian."

"Your hair is beautiful, Axton. And it makes you look smart. They're just jealous."

My hair was not beautiful. Even I knew that. The kids at school were right: my hair looked like the end of a dirty Q-tip. I had begged my mom to let me grow it long, but she refused. Every six weeks she dragged me to her friend Kathy's daughter's salon, hovering in the corner like a boxing coach, encouraging her to keep chopping. Apparently, when I was very little, I would howl if Mom tried to brush my hair, so it had to go. I was older now, but the mandate remained.

"You hated that school, too, Mom," I said. She had found her keys and was gripping them tightly in her hand. "You always say that."

"Let me talk to your dad." She sighed.

"He'll say it's too expensive to go anywhere else!"

My mother looked at me in tacit agreement.

"Honey, I have to go. We'll talk about this later."

I was back in my room before the storm door closed. My *Sweet Valley High* book was poised atop my pillow like a butterfly. I flopped down next to it. With no phone, and no friends nearby, I whiled away the long summer day lost in its thin pages.

* * *

But then a miracle happened. A series of miracles, actually. Mom ran into Dennis, an old Portland acquaintance. It just so happened that his daughter was happily attending Heritage Hall, a Christian school in Muncie. Mom mentioned my disdain for East Jay, and Dennis had urged her to consider sending me

Mom and me—and our matching haircuts—before the first-grade Christmas play.

to his daughter's school. He said that I could catch a ride to school with his wife (who worked there) and children every day. When Mom consulted Dad, he was predictably contrary. The tuition was steep—$400 a month—and I'd have to attend a slew of religious events and classes. But Mom coerced him, probably by recounting her own miserable junior high experience, and reminding him that investing in their only child's education was a worthy expense. We never really got Dad's seal of approval, but a few weeks later, Mom and I celebrated my acceptance to Heritage Hall.

It was an adjustment, and not the easy one I thought it would be. I began waking up at 4:00 a.m. so that Mom could drive me to the Shepherds'—the family that was going to give me a ride to Muncie. At the Shepherds', we would exchange tired hellos as I transferred my things to their blue sedan. The sun wasn't even a hint on the horizon when we set out on the hour-long drive. Mrs. Shepherd was a preschool teacher at Heritage Hall, and her daughter, Scarlett, was in sixth grade there. The son, David, was a junior. As an eighth grader I felt a kinship with neither of them, just smiled when they cracked jokes or fixed my eyes on my lap when they talked about family stuff.

In school, I was behind. My public school education had not prepared me for Heritage Hall's academic rigor. I had to get tutoring to get caught up. Tutoring sessions were as foreign to me as the long skirts I was made to wear. In the afternoons, Mrs. Shepherd's car deposited me behind the Portland Office Supply, where Mom now had a one-room office for her tax-preparation business, and where I would promptly start hours' worth of homework. The circles under my eyes grew dark but I was glad to be away from the bullies and monotony of East Jay.

As the new girl in a small school, everyone was very interested in me—what my old school was like, what kinds of animals we raised on our farm, and when I had accepted Jesus Christ as my Savior. I struggled with the last question. My Catholic baptism meant that, technically, I had been saved—I thought— though in catechism classes we didn't really talk about it like that. Mainly we learned about the saints and the church's history and the major rules we needed to follow. Before my acceptance to Heritage Hall, Mom and Dad met with the head-master, a stern man aptly named Mr. Ice, who assured them the religious differences would not be a concern. But apparently when Mom's friend Dennis had vouched for my acceptance to Heritage Hall, he had also made mention of my off-brand salvation. That seed of information, planted before I even arrived at the school, had taken root; concern bloomed among the teachers, Mrs. Shepherd among them. Morning dynamics grew uncomfortable. The Christian radio station got louder, and conversations turned more often to Jesus. When Mrs. Shepherd approached Mom about my salvation, Mom thought she was doing me a favor by mentioning our Catholicism.

My hair and my academic prowess had made me an outcast at East Jay, and now my casual Catholicism was threatening to do the same at Heritage Hall. So that fall, when a girl in my class named Nikki started asking me to hang out, I was thrilled. Nikki's mom also worked at the school (sometimes it seemed only my parents weren't employed there) and her dad was a pilot. The first time I went over to her house, I'm not sure if I was more awestruck by the prop plane in their backyard or the pinball machine in their barn. After a few get-togethers, Nikki invited me to go witnessing with her; I jumped at the opportunity. I didn't know what witnessing was, but that seemed irrelevant.

At the end of ninth period, Nikki led me to a school van, where a dozen kids already sat with their book bags between their legs, chatting and laughing. We took the last seats on the front bench, Nikki closing the door behind us. The air inside the van was heavy with the scent of Freon and rubber floor mats. I closed my eyes. I felt Nikki's shoulder pressed against mine. I couldn't remember ever feeling a part of such a big, buoyant group. Gratitude for my mother swelled inside me.

The van rumbled through the worn-out, working-class neighborhoods of Muncie and came to a stop in a cul-de-sac. The adult—someone's mom, I think—who had been sitting in the passenger seat slid open the van door. Everyone tumbled out; first Nikki, then me, then nine or ten other sets of feet hit the pavement.

"Do you want me to get you a sheet?" Nikki nodded her head toward a small stack of papers in the adults' hands.

"Um. No, that's okay." We couldn't be caroling. It was late summer.

The group of kids moved in unison like a swarm of swallows, the adults staying behind. We walked up to the first house, a wool-colored ranch with a beat-up storm door. I fell back, stopping a few yards from the front stoop. My class-mates brushed past me eagerly. When a boy I had seen in the cafeteria extended his finger to ring the doorbell, the edges of my vision went blurry. Everything suddenly felt very wrong. Since I was a child, I had been told not to talk to strangers. But since the mail started to go missing, I had been told not to talk to anyone.

"Hello, ma'am, we're from Heritage Hall Christian School and we're here to talk to you about the love of Jesus Christ, our Lord and Savior."

So that's what witnessing was.

While my classmates extolled the virtues of their intimate re-lationship with Jesus from house to house, I dutifully brought up the rear. Sometimes I would make eye contact with the person at the door; sometimes they were in their bathrobe, sometimes less. Sometimes I felt like they were looking through me, could tell I wasn't one of the angelic kids before them. At every house, I noticed the mailbox, clipped with outgoing bills or overflowing with circulars. We marched until the sun went down; my jaw ached from the clutching.

Back in the van, Nikki filled out the back row, leaving me to sit awkwardly up front with two girls who, I noticed with a pang of despair, wore matching friendship bracelets.

That night, as I forwent sleep to get my homework done, I felt ragged with defeat. My heart hurt and my eyes burned. It wasn't all bad, I told myself. Good or bad at witnessing, I had been something even better: invited.

* * *

At Heritage Hall, the eighth-grade class—all sixteen students— took a spring trip to Washington, DC, each year. As a fund-raiser for the trip, parents took turns making cookies that were sold in the lunch line on Fridays. The stacks of quarters generated from the cookies paid for the charter bus and cheap hotel rooms just outside the District.

My mother was not a baker. In fact, she despised any activity that required her to turn on the stove. So when I told her about DC and about the fund-raiser, she was annoyed.

"I'd rather just give you the money. Can I do that?"

"Mom, everyone else's parents make cookies. Can we just make cookies?" I had broached the subject the weekend before the Friday I needed to deliver them to school. I would have asked Dad but his harvest-time chores were holding him hostage out back.

"Fine," she responded curtly, as if she were the teenager.

The next Thursday night, Mom lugged out her old food processor, its once white exterior yellowed from age and neglect. She said making cookies in the food processor would be faster, easier. Thirty minutes later I grimaced as Mom pulled the sad, muddy squares from the oven. Almost like graham crackers, but smaller and oddly shaped. How was it possible that my mother could make even the most mundane things embarrassing? I said nothing, just bagged up the cookies—no more than two per Ziploc bag, per Mom's insistence—and took them to school the next morning. I held them tightly, in a curled-up grocery sack, on the long ride to Muncie. My salvation was still the undercurrent of our conversation; the Christian radio had reached a deafening pitch.

At school I delivered the cookies to Mr. McKee's desk before Bible class started. I took my normal seat in the back, put my tired head down, and began quietly reciting the verses I had memorized over the weekend.

I heard the swish of wet shoes as kids shuffled in around me. The familiar squeak of Mr. McKee's dress shoes straightened me up. Mr. McKee was a lanky man with immaculately trimmed brown hair. I watched as he strolled to his desk, his eyes locked on my pathetic bag of cookies. I was suddenly aware of my heartbeat.

"And *who* brought these?" he said with a grin, holding them up for everyone to behold. My mother's cookies hung in the air like a sack of golf balls. There were snickers. I winced.

"They're too small," he continued. "We can't charge fifty cents for these. Who brought them? They won't work for lunch." Fifteen heads turned toward my desk.

"Me." My voice was tiny.

Mr. McKee's shoes squeaked all the way to my desk. Heat blossomed in my cheeks.

"Tell your mom these are too small, Axton." He set the bag on my desk with a dozen humiliating thuds. "Now, are you ready to recite your verses?"

I threw the cookies away in the girls' bathroom after class.

There was still another crisis to resolve and I couldn't waste my time with any more cookies. That had been only the first hurdle on this sprint. It plagued me all day: how would we call the next family on the fund-raising phone tree without a home phone? Earlier in the year, we had been handed a form with names of the sixteen families and phone numbers to call. Mom's office number was on it . . . but we weren't going to drive to Mom's office to make the call, were we? If so, people might figure out we weren't calling from a home phone and realize we didn't have one. Then people would make fun of me, just like they did at East Jay. When I told Mom about the phone tree, she seemed just as concerned about our public perception as I did. Even better, she already had a solution in mind. That evening we drove to the strip mall just north of the 76 station in Portland. The Cellular Connection was lit up bright like a beacon, its glow soothing my shattered nerves. For the first time all day, I felt like everything might work out. The woman working the counter was helpful, and soon we had what we needed— a Nokia flip phone that opened to expose its oversized, spongy buttons. We chose a thirty-dollar calling card, too, that would be good for the whole month.

At home, Mom moved a stool from the counter in front of the china cabinet across the room. The cabinet was full of Grandma's old dishes, the ones with the pinecones that we used only for holidays. She plugged in the bulky power pack and traced the cord with her fingers to the phone, which she placed carefully on top of the stool. After adding the thirty-dollar prepaid minutes from the card to the phone, she backed away to admire it like a work of art. We smiled at each other.

"Make your call," she said. "Just try to keep it under a minute."

"I will."

Before she left the kitchen she stopped in the doorway.

"Did my cookies sell out?" she asked, beaming with mock pride.

"Actually, Mom"—I kept my eyes on the phone in my hands—"can you make some different cookies? Mr. McKee said they were too small." I could sense my mother's smile turn into a scowl.

"I did my part," she said, leaving the kitchen, bound for her well-worn seat on the couch.

SEVEN

ASKING FOR HELP FROM my mother for school-related issues wasn't new, and sometimes I got the help I wanted. Earlier that year, I was in living room with mom begging to have her get me out of four days with kids I hardly knew at a camp I had never been to, attending chapel for a religion that I wasn't a part of. This was not an optional activity; it was required of all junior and senior high students at Heritage Hall. It was like someone had designed an experience based solely on things that made me uncomfortable.

"It's their house, Axton. Gotta play by their rules." That was it. That was all Mom had offered me. I hesitated to go all in on my protest. Mom and Dad were fighting nearly every day about money, and my tuition was high on their docket. Complaining too much would give my dad more fuel and I still felt indebted to Mom for getting me out of East Jay. I'd suffer through it.

The Indiana heat and humidity was high on the late August day we departed for camp. I felt a tinge of nervousness travel up my spine when the powder-blue church bus lurched out of the parking lot. It was late summer, which in Indiana means a persistent, swampy heat. Every one of the bus's windows were pushed down, creating a vortex of hot wind that parted my hair at strange angles and tossed the curls up into irregular bursts. It was too loud to say anything to Nikki, who was sitting next to me by the window, cornfields behind her in a blur, so I just stared ahead.

Camp Crosley was a YMCA camp in North Webster, in the northern part of the state that's speckled with small lakes. It was an unremarkable complex: a shallow woods, a mess hall, a smattering of cabins. When we arrived, I followed the flock of eighth-grade girls to our cabin, our bags and suitcases bumping against our legs as we walked. The inside of the cabin seemed to swallow the light from the gaping front door, and bunk beds that jutted out from the walls made a maze of the remaining floor space. I found my way to an unoccupied bed and exhaled with relief when Nikki, with her tote bag, claimed the one next to mine. We hurried to the bathhouse to use the toilets and to tame our windblown hair with water that smelled of sulfur. It was a squat building with ventilation fans humming. The cramped interior smelled caustic and spiders had built their gauzy homes in each vacant corner.

The days were mercifully busy. At breakfast, a buffet stacked with more cereal boxes than I had ever seen open at one time flanked the long aisles of picnic tables. We'd clamor for our plastic bowls and circle until we found the sugar-dusted kind we wanted. It had been a while since I'd had my choice; the cupboards at home were growing increasingly sparse. Morning chapel was an hour, followed by outdoor activities I actually enjoyed. We were allowed to change out of our long skirts for water sports and paddleboats. Afternoon chapel was the worst part of the day. Two sweaty hours of fire-and-brimstone sermons; the palms of my hands stuck to the pew.

On Wednesday morning, I woke early and watched the sun rise against the cabin wall, satisfied that I had made it through the first two days. *Tomorrow,* I thought, *I get to go home.* I sailed through breakfast, chapel, and a paddleboat foray. Some girls tried to playfully tip over my paddleboat and I had to yell at them to stop. I was the only thirteen-year-old on the trip who didn't know how to swim. Lunch was more salty camp fare and then we all lined up for chapel.

I found my usual spot in the back and watched as the rest of the junior high and high school students filed in. Some of the girls still had wet hair, and everyone's face glowed red from our long days in the sun. Above us were exposed beams of dark wood framing small slivers of skylights that admitted a tantalizing amount of the afternoon. The stage was set with a chair and lectern, though the pastor preferred to hover menacingly near the front row, walking up and down the aisle when he needed to drive home a point. I wasn't a fan of his sermons; he was a yeller. His round face and bald head would grow ruddy and splotched as he described the horrors of hell.

Fifteen minutes into the service, I had drifted off into a daydream. In my reverie, it was the next day and I was home with Chunx, my beloved cat, in my sunny bedroom. I sat on the red carpet as he wove in and out of my limbs, thrilled at my return.

"But if YOU are not saved! YOU will spend eternity in hell." The pastor's stubby index finger was aimed at me like a rifle. Dozens of tanned faces turned toward me. I swallowed my breath. Blood pulsed in the tips of my fingers.

And just as quickly I was looking at the back of his white robe and heads rotating again to the front of the room. I felt Nikki look over at me but kept my eyes fastened on the stage.

One minute passed. Two.

I was breathing again. Three. Four.

But now I was shaking, a wave of nausea cresting in my throat.

Five minutes. Six.

I had to get out of there.

"I don't feel good. I have to go outside," I whispered to Nikki. She immediately got up and walked over to Mrs. Ice, the head-master's wife and eighth-grade girls' chaperone. But I couldn't wait. On trembling legs I staggered toward the door at the back of the hall. My body pitched into the afternoon and I caught myself on the wooden railing just outside the entrance. Mrs. Ice appeared beside me like an apparition.

"Axton, hold on." She put her hand on my back. "Let's pray, and you'll feel better."

The ground below was getting fuzzy like a broken VCR tape, so I closed my eyes as Mrs. Ice asked God to enter my body and give me relief. Her prayer (which may have been brief but felt like an epic poem) was unsuccessful. Maybe, I thought, maybe I was dying.

"You have to let me go home," I said, still staring at the ground.

"Now, come on, Axton, you're going to feel better real soon. You just need to rest a bit. Let's go over to the teachers' cabin and sit you down."

I had no idea how my legs would make it that far.

"Please just call my mom. We have a phone; please call her— I have to go home."

"Let's go sit down for a bit and you'll feel better," she said. I gritted my teeth and began to shuffle with her across the grass.

The teachers' cabin was nice. There were couches and a refrigerator and the interior felt bright and airy. Breathing was taking some serious concentration, but when I looked up to find my way to a seat, I saw my English teacher, Mrs. Brown. A tiny burst of relief knocked against the wall of my chest. Mrs. Brown was, by far, the coolest teacher at Heritage Hall. At Halloween, she actually decorated her classroom for the "pagan" holiday. If I was about to die, everyone else would circle around me and pray, but Mrs. Brown would call the ambulance. Now her kind face beckoned me to the couch at the far end of the cabin.

"Axton, what's wrong?" she said softly.

"I can't breathe. I think I am going to throw up. I want to go home."

"Why don't you sip on some water and try to breathe very slowly."

I nodded. But inside I raged. Every cell in my body was in revolt. And nobody cared.

Hours passed. Teachers orbited, taking turns sitting with me. When they asked how they could help, I said the same thing: "Please just let me go home."

"Home is three hours away—it's too late," Mrs. Ice said, well into the evening, signaling that perhaps my requests were starting to get somewhere.

"We live in Portland, so it's only two hours. My mom will come and get me. Please call her." I thought about the Nokia perched on the stool by the pinecone china. "Please."

I was escorted to the mess hall by a small cadre of teachers. I thought they were going to try to make me eat. Instead, I was ushered over to Mr. Habeggar, the principal. He pulled out the steel folding chair across from his, and I collapsed into it weakly.

"We called your mom—" Relief muted whatever came next. "—ing a new school is hard, I know. I have family in Portland, and I know how tight-knit it can be."

Soon I was in Mr. Habeggar's car, in front of the IGA in North Webster. It was well past closing time but the lights were still on, casting a yellow glow on the bags of softener salt stacked up beside the automatic doors. When Mom's two-toned black-and-silver truck pulled into the parking lot a few minutes later, I was outside before she came to a stop.

The adults exchanged concerned pleasantries while I nestled into the passenger seat of Mom's truck. My muscles throbbed and my teeth radiated pain. I had heard the phrase "strung out" before and suddenly knew exactly what it meant. When Mom got in the truck, she pushed her palm against my forehead. "What's wrong with you?" she said, her face contorted with worry. I just shook my head.

Wednesday had become Thursday and the sickness, the flu, or whatever it was that had permeated my body in that chapel, gripped me tight until the familiar lights of Fort Wayne appeared on the horizon.

EIGHT

IT WAS THE SAME YEAR, my eighth-grade year, when closed curtains became a hard-and-fast rule in our house. Around that time, I was instructed to never answer the door, even if I knew who it was. After the mail went missing and the phone got shut off, a vulnerability that wasn't there before seemed to permeate our daily lives. Anything and anyone outside those drapes, those limestone walls, possessed intentions we could never be sure of. We could only trust one another. My dad, becoming increasingly convinced Mom was right that someone was out to get us, entrusted me with keeping the property safe. He started saying things like "If someone crosses the gate, they're yours. You have to protect the property."

At fourteen, I became hypervigilant, always on guard. At the end of each day, my neck and shoulders would ache with fatigue from long hours of keen attentiveness; I heard each passing car, searched the eyes of every strange and familiar face at the store. That my no-nonsense father and brazen, spitfire mother had failed to protect us only convinced me they needed my help. Paranoia became an obligation, a twisted kind of duty to my family.

The front of our house.

In the evenings after school, I would sit down at my particle-board desk and spread out my homework like an elaborate meal. I divided the piles by subject and always started with the easiest, which meant a lot of late nights wrestling with math problems. While I worked, I secretly pulled my drapes open a crack, so that I could keep an eye on the front of the property. With Dad out back doing chores and Mom always on the couch, someone needed to keep watch.

The sun was low in the sky when the white utility truck pulled gently onto the shoulder in front of the house. Its passenger-side door said *Ohio Valley Gas*. It idled for a moment, and then a tall man in an official-looking uniform got out and walked around to the back of the truck. My mind worked fast while he sorted through a toolbox.

Ohio Valley Gas was our gas company, so that checked out. This man's gray outfit seemed legitimate, and the man himself almost looked familiar to me—maybe I had seen him in town?

He had parked in the right place—the gas meter was just a few feet from his truck, near the highway. Everything seemed okay except the time of day. It was late, almost eight o'clock. I couldn't remember anyone reading the meter after dinner before.

Mom and Dad needed to know.

I pushed back my chair and walked briskly into the living room. The TV was casting blue-and-purple shadows on my mother's tired face.

"Mom. There's a man from the gas company out front."

"Okay, Axton," she said with a disinterested tone.

"Don't you think it's late for that?"

"Not really. He's probably just reading the meter."

I didn't have time for my mother to catch up with my suspicion. I headed for the barn.

Thankfully, without me having to say much, Dad was on the same wavelength. After I told him about the service call he looked with a furrowed brow toward the front yard. Quickly, he began walking toward the front of the house. I cut a hard angle to the back door and shot inside the house to monitor the conversation from my room.

Leaning forward with my elbow on the windowsill, I watched as my dad approached the utility worker, who was already at the meter. He had a metal clipboard in his hands and was bent over at a ninety-degree angle. Surrounded by gravel, the gas meter was a clay-colored thing that emerged from the ground at knee height. I had often glanced at it from my bedroom window and worried—what if someone slid off the road and hit it? Would it cause an explosion? Now I watched and hoped it didn't cause a different kind of crisis than the one I had envisioned.

My father's body language was polite but insistent. He kept his arms crossed over his chest as if he was protecting himself from another unwanted intrusion. The utility man was gesticulating with his clipboard, at times pointing to it with his pen. The tightness in my heart lessened just slightly when I saw him smile and nod his head at my dad in a familiar way. Still, the conversation lasted much too long for anything good to be happening.

My elbows were beginning to ache when I watched the two men shake hands in the disappearing sunlight. I moved slowly from my window to the orange-carpeted hallway adjacent to the living room so that I appeared in its entryway when Dad stepped inside. My mother looked up from the TV at me and then him.

"Well. He came out here to shut the gas off," he said, "for nonpayment on our property in New Corydon. New Corydon? You know anything about that?" He looked at Mom, who rolled her eyes.

"Of course not. It must be part of the identity theft," she said, her voice finally full of concern.

"Luckily the guy recognized me from work—I guess he shops at the store a lot. He thinks we graduated together, too. He says he knows we aren't the type to not pay our bills, said it must be a big misunderstanding." My dad pushed a hand through his graying hair. He sighed with a mix of relief and confusion.

"But Bobby and Mary live up in New Corydon," Mom said.

"Uh-huh. So?" The TV was still blaring, and neither of them seemed to notice I was standing there. Neither of them seemed particularly grateful that I had spotted the utility truck in the first place.

"It would make sense if they were behind this whole thing. You know Mary's been convicted of welfare fraud," Mom said aloud, theorizing about potential perpetrators.

Bobby was Dad's cousin and Mary was his wife. They had

lived in the northern part of the county in an old schoolhouse before they moved to New Corydon. Bobby had a mess of deep red hair atop his head and a face that seemed to be perpetually sunburned. Mary was long and lean, and I never saw her when her coarse blond hair wasn't pulled back in a tight bun. Her teeth were in rough shape; some were missing, some were chipped or cracked. They had three children, two girls and a little boy, and the girls also showed chickens at the county fair.

Outside of seeing them during the fair, Bobby and Mary didn't come around much. Once, Bobby called Dad up saying he needed firewood to heat the schoolhouse they lived in, so Dad invited him to come forage in the woods behind our house. Mom threw a fit, yelling that she didn't want Bobby anywhere near us. She made me hide in my room with the lights off so that the kids wouldn't know I was home.

I guessed it was possible that Bobby and Mary were behind the identity theft, but not likely. Neither of them seemed particularly savvy enough to pull off such a long and coordinated scheme. Mom had said that Mary had once been convicted of welfare fraud, but even if that was true, her conviction negated the idea that she was skilled at this kind of deceit. Also, Bobby and Mary were different from us—harried, scrappy, unmoved by convention—but they weren't *mean*. And whoever was doing this stuff to us was, in my estimation, decidedly mean.

"I don't know, Pam. I'm ready for this all to be over."

"I'll go to the police tomorrow and tell them about this new thing. Maybe they'll go up to New Corydon and ask your cousin some questions."

Dad didn't respond, just made his way through the living room. Mom reassigned her gaze to the console television in the corner.

As my father went out back to finish his twilit chores, I returned to my room and slumped down in front of my books. I pulled an eraser from the bunny tin on my desk; I would need it for the algebra homework I had been putting off. Just then the distant hum of a car engine approached until headlights illuminated the ash trees in the yard. I held my breath as it passed without slowing, then leaned forward to watch as its taillights disappeared into the night like bonfire embers.

NINE

Maybe Mom told the cops about the latest incident, maybe she didn't. As a child, I wasn't privy to many of my parents' conversations, though I assumed Mom took care of the issue with the gas company at some point; the gas stayed on, anyway. We didn't talk about New Corydon again. Like most of my mother's theories, the one about Bobby and Mary seemed to come and go without any deeper consideration. It also hinged upon people from Dad's circle, as her conspiracies often did. Mom disliked virtually every member of Dad's family, and as a child, I thought she had good reason to.

My father's childhood was not a happy one. He spoke of it rarely, but I could picture the modest brown two-story home he had described a few times, facing a desolate country road outside of Bellfountain, Indiana. The town was hardly more than a crossroads and a church in eastern Jay County, but it was a cheap place to live with industry nearby. My grandmother, Barb, found work in a factory assembling TV sensors the size of a nickel. Dad's father, Leonard, was a welder.

The family wasn't rich, but they had enough to get by. Unlike

Mom's family, no one in Dad's drank heavily or wore shiny jewelry or fell off boat docks in the middle of the night. The Betzes were just normal, blue-collar folks. That my grandmother was possessed with some kind of awful rage seemed out of place in this otherwise quintessential image of Americana, and made what I knew about her that much more sinister.

It was probably Mom who first told me about Grandma Betz's violent streak. About my dad crawling out of windows and climbing the TV antenna tower to get away from her in the middle of the night. About the beatings with blunt objects and broomsticks. About Dad keeping his younger sister, my aunt Lisa, with him at all times to protect her from their mother's fury. Dad seldom spoke of his upbringing, but he did give me a piece of advice about interacting with Grandma: "Never turn your back to her."

Dad's dad was not mean, but scared like his children, and so an accomplice in his wife's tyranny. Leonard also delivered beatings at Barb's behest.

As soon as he could, Dad left home.

As soon as Lisa followed, Barb left Leonard.

There's a funny anecdote my parents used to pass around. On the day that Barb changed the locks on Leonard to let him know it was over, Lisa had come over to tell Mom the news. Four at the time, I listened intently to the fresh gossip, radically confused by what I was hearing. I thought moms and dads, husbands and wives, were indivisible entities, two inextricable gears of the same machine. When my father arrived home from his shift at the grocery that day, I greeted him, distraught, at the door.

"Grandma Betz is a divorcer!" I shrieked.

Recalling my toddler's moral outrage is the only thing that will get my dad to smile when his mother is the topic of conversation.

Leonard moved in with Lisa after the split, despite her already taxing roles of a new wife and mother. After Grandpa Elliott died and we moved into his house, my parents invited Grandpa Betz to take up in the green-and-white mobile home we had vacated. He hemmed and hawed for years, but Mom and Dad persisted. One day when I was wasting time while Mom worked at her office, she handed me a newly cut key.

"Walk this to Lisa's house," she said. "It's time Grandpa gets out of there and comes to live with us."

As I stalked the half-dozen blocks to Lisa's, I wondered why my mom was so adamant. I figured the extra help for Dad would be nice, and even though I was old enough to stay on my own now, having another adult around might make things a little safer. While Dad and Grandpa had slowly repaired their relationship after years of abuse-by-proxy, Grandpa Betz had never taken any real interest in me. Whereas Grandpa Elliott bought me Double Stuf Oreos and let me watch cartoons, I couldn't remember one time Leonard had given me a gift. I guessed he couldn't really afford to, since he more or less spent every cent he had gambling.

In fact, Leonard had a pretty rigid gambling schedule. He went to the American Legion daily. On Wednesdays and Saturdays, he was at the Legion helping run bingo. On Tuesdays he went to the Moose Lodge. One Monday a month, he went to the Forty and Eight club, another veterans' group. All that gambling never amounted to much, and if it did, the winnings were gone before he could even brag about them.

The new key seemed to convince Grandpa it was okay to move into the backyard, because pretty soon he and his scant belongings appeared out there. It was odd seeing him in our old home, the first place I remembered as ours. My parents had had the mobile home custom built in the late seventies when they came home to care for Mom's mom. As far as mobile homes go, it was high-end. Wood paneling lined the interior and dainty, off-white curtains fluttered in its windows. There was a raised dining room separate from the kitchen, and the living room extended out from the main frame. Because Mom and Dad weren't planning on having kids, the second bedroom, the one that became mine, was smaller than the bathroom. It did have a built-in corner shelf where I could arrange my cat figurines.

We took good care of that mobile home, Dad and me. Every year, he'd weatherproof the roof, climbing up on a ladder with a ten-gallon bucket of what looked like silver paint. I'd stay down below to hand him tools and rags when he called for them. In the winter, we'd have to weatherproof the exposed pipes against the oncoming freeze. Since Dad discovered his dormant claustrophobia under the mobile home, and because I was smaller, this part was my job. I'd shimmy my body between the cold frame and the hard ground, one hand clinging to the heat tape to reach the outlet underneath the mobile home to plug it in. With my hair and clothes collecting dirt and dead grass, I'd ensure the heat tape was securely plugged in and working before shimmying my way back out from under the mobile home.

The back side of the farm and our mobile home.

By the time Grandpa Betz moved in, the mobile home was nearly twenty years old, but still in prime condition. My parents let him have it rent-free, as long as he helped out on the farm and occasionally took care of things at our house. I was thrilled when he moved in because it meant I no longer had to cut the grass. It wasn't quite cartoons and cookies, but I counted it as a small gift.

* * *

One night, not long after Grandpa came to stay, I was at my desk when I heard a car pull into the driveway. I had been laboring over a particularly heavy load of homework and had only vaguely registered the sound of the approaching car. Since the utility truck, every other car on every other night had rumbled past our house, each one revealing to me that this paranoia was a good way to never get anything done. I had let my guard down, and now there was a sheriff's cruiser in the driveway.

"Mom!" I yelled before I even got to the living room.

"What?" Her eyes were waiting for my body to appear before her. The TV was on a sitcom she liked, the laugh track conflicting with the gravity of my news.

"The sheriff is here."

If she was worried, my mother didn't show it. She sat up a little straighter, but didn't stand. Dad, however, who was in the kitchen, went out the back door so that he could walk around to the gate. The gate that had come to stand between good and evil, safety and harm.

I trained my eyes on Mom, who was now sitting quietly with her arms crossed, eyes pointed in the direction of the gate. We couldn't see much, but we could hear the two men greet each other. I couldn't bear it another second.

Our house was built in 1952, so my closet wasn't exactly roomy. I had hidden there before, when I was home alone during the summers. I parted my dress shirts and spun my body around, lowering my back against the wall. As my eyes adjusted to the dark, I felt around for shoeboxes, stuffed animals—anything to conceal my feet and legs. And then I listened.

I could hear the murmur of conversation; I could hear surprise, then outrage infusing my father's muffles. I closed my eyes tightly and pressed my forehead to my knees. *Please*, I thought, *please make this stop.*

And then it did stop. The conversation was done and I heard a car door slam, an engine start. I pushed my way through the tower of plush things and boxes, half crawling until I hit the hallway.

"They were here to arrest you, Pam!" My father's voice was as angry as I had heard it. "Check deception. Bad checks at the Portland Walmart."

That was impossible. Mom thought we were too good to be Walmart shoppers and often said as much, while lamenting there was nowhere else in Portland to buy clothes or household stuff.

My mother gasped. I stared at the floor.

"I told him about the identity theft, that there's just no way you would, or we would, ever do something like that. But this has gone on long enough. This has to stop." He stood above her with his arms crossed.

Yes, I thought, *this has to stop.* Whoever was doing this to us was now pretending to be Mom in broad daylight, mere miles from our house. This person was brazen. They clearly thought they were above the law. My stomach spun like wind chimes in a storm. *Make this stop.*

"If I knew how to make it stop, I would have done that a long time ago!" My mother was defensive. "I'm doing everything I can but it seems like whoever this is has all the information they need now."

"I've had it. I can't live like this anymore." My chest expanded; Dad was finally going to make this all go away. I held my breath as I awaited his big idea.

But instead of a heroic solution, or some kind of reassuring gesture, my father walked through the living room, the kitchen, and out the back door. I was beginning to understand: He couldn't live like *this* anymore—in *this* house, with *this* turmoil, with *this* family. So as much as he could, he was living outside, at work, with the animals.

A commercial for face wash came on, concealing the wounded silence Mom and I shared.

It felt like our lives were swirling in concentric circles. Live next door to one grandpa until he dies, and then move the other grandpa in. Watch the cars pass left to right, left to right, left to right. Put out one fire at the front door while another burns in New Corydon, at Walmart, in some place we can't even imagine.

TEN

ALL THE WHILE, I tried my best to put on a happy front. At the beginning of ninth grade I was elected class secretary. It was a triumphant moment for me, marred only by the fact that it wasn't exactly what I had wanted. I had wanted to be class president. But weeks before, as I studied the requirements of that role, buried deep in its stated academic requirements and behavioral standards, I had stumbled upon an infuriating disqualifier: *must be male.* So I ran for the lesser office and won. Despite the patriarchal roadblock, the victory made me feel a genuine affection for my classmates; they were kind and inclusive, even if their parents were not.

Part of my responsibility as secretary was to lead the entire junior and senior high in reciting the Christian Pledge of Allegiance during morning chapel: *I pledge allegiance to the Christian flag, and to the Savior for whose Kingdom it stands; one Savior, crucified, risen, and coming again, with life and liberty for all who believe.* Each class secretary took a turn in leading the junior and senior high students through this pledge. I seemed to be the only student who noticed the irony that I—the casual Catholic—was now conducting the daily recitation. I felt like a phony at the front of the room.

During the first few weeks of the school year, we were told to prepare for a day-trip to Indianapolis, to attend a large Baptist revival. To my mind, that meant a lot of loud and red-faced men screaming about the impending rapture with equal parts mean-ness and glee. The participation slip noted that students unable to join for a compelling reason could opt out, but would need to come to school that day anyway, for an alternate assignment. I hardly finished reading the paragraph before marching to the main office.

I found Headmaster Ice at his desk; he smiled grimly when I came in. He was a hulking, balding man. Gray hair framed the apex of his head like a halo.

"I can't go on the Indianapolis trip," I said, harnessing all my confidence. "We'll get back too late and my parents won't be able to pick me up."

"Mmm-hmm" was his response.

"So may I please have the alternate assignment?"

Mr. Ice took off his glasses and straightened a stack of papers in front of him. "You know, Miss Betz, we've dealt with people like you before."

The air around me seemed to buzz. I wasn't sure what that was supposed to mean, or how to respond, so I muttered a thank-you and left quickly. Later that night, I told Dad what Mr. Ice had said.

"Well, that son of a bitch hasn't dealt with someone like *me* before," he growled.

His tolerance—as well as my own—for the school's aggressive indoctrination was waning.

"I hate to say it," Mom said, "but it's only going to get worse as you get older. They clearly have an expectation that you will become a Baptist, despite what they promised."

We were sitting in the living room around the television. Maybe it was because there were four hundred tuition dollars a month at stake, but for once, Mom had turned down the volume.

"I'm learning so much, though," I said. It was true. I was miles ahead of my public school counterparts. *And* I was well liked enough to hold a student government office.

"Then you'll need to play by their rules," Mom said. It was something she mentioned a lot—"their house," "their way," "their rules." I was still a young teenager, but I was growing weary of everybody's rules.

In the end, I decided to leave Heritage Hall. With so much uncertainty and conflict at home, I didn't have it in me to battle pushy adults about my salvation. I just wanted to disappear back into the mass of kids at public school. I just wanted everyone to leave me alone.

The next week Mom and I met with a guidance counselor— he had been Dad's thirty years before—at Jay County High School. It was homecoming week and the front office was decked out with inane decorations. A video of a boy dancing in a hula skirt played on a television monitor. At the time, the school was rumored to have the highest rate of teen pregnancy in the state. Over the course of the morning, we carefully picked out my classes, making sure to set me up for the honors track. I would need to get through gym, but then things would get better. I had been telling myself that for so long that sometimes I actually believed it.

ELEVEN

WHEN I WAS YOUNG, probably too young to be on a three-wheeler, my father and I would ride around the woods behind the farm for entire afternoons. The immense tract of beech, ash, and maple trees was set so far back from the road it was easy to pretend nothing else existed for hours on end. Together, we built trails and ponds, and we built a bridge over the creek connecting the north side of the woods to the south. Everyone in town begged Dad to open his woods up for hunting, but he refused. Instead he liked to watch the deer saunter through the forest, licking the salt blocks he had laid out like presents. We were happy to share our quiet haven with them.

Back then, my father never came home from work without a treat for me. He would walk in the door and stand as still as a mannequin, a delighted smile across his face, until I figured out in which pocket he had hidden some peculiar item from the store. Then I would accompany him outside, where we would get to work feeding the animals, riding the three-wheeler, or cleaning animal pens.

Mom had always been protective. If she saw a story on the

news about a kidnapping, she would spend days warning me about all the bad people out there, the ones who steal kids from their nighttime bedrooms, from the bus stop. As the identity theft began to claim more and more of our collective consciousness, Mom wanted me outside less than she had before, in the barn and especially in the woods. She said that the person had stolen so much from us already, that they likely had a vendetta against us, and it wasn't a stretch to think that they might steal me, too. She said she had heard about people who drove up and down US 27, looking to snatch kids from their yards, that there were strangers lurking in the woods. After hearing that the identity thief had the audacity to impersonate my mother, I was beginning to think she was right.

Dad and I spent fewer sunlit hours together out back, and I was getting too old for grocery store treats. Slowly, our tether unwound, until it felt as if all we had left in common were the crimes committed against us. We were like plaintiffs in the same trial.

It was early winter. The roads were already stained salt white. My father had picked me up from school after his shift at the grocery store. We said little on the twenty-minute drive home and I fixed my eyes on the fields whirring by. A cold wind snapped across the stubbly remains of last summer's soybeans and corn, but it was mercifully sunny out.

When we pulled into the driveway, we both seemed to see it at the same time. The long, yellow door tag. Waving slightly in the breeze like it knew we were home. I thought I could hear my dad's jaw tightening. I took a deep breath and prepared myself for a new disaster.

The power had been turned off. For nonpayment. My father ripped the tag from the door and stormed inside with purpose.

Mom was still at work. I followed a few steps behind, through the eerily quiet house—no clocks ticking, no appliances humming—and out back to the yard. The icy blades of grass broke under our feet.

Dad never made it to the mobile home; Grandpa was outside feeding the dogs. "Were you here when this happened?" my father asked, fist balled and holding up the yellow tag for context. "How did this get here?"

My grandfather, seemingly oblivious to my father's heightened emotional state and with a shrug of his shoulders, said simply, "The guy said he needed in. So I let him in."

"We've been over this," my father insisted. "Don't you *ever* let anyone in without calling me first. This"—he waved the tag for effect—"is a mistake. This is not for us."

I didn't stick around to hear the rest of the lecture. If anyone had internalized Dad's warnings, it was me. It had, after all, been only a few months since the incident with the knife.

I had been home alone on a school holiday the day the beat-up black van came to a stop outside our house. I hated being trapped in the dark house alone all day, and that morning, even Grandpa was gone, doing something with one of the veterans groups. I had just sat down to flip endlessly through daytime television when, through a gap in the heavy drapes, I watched with horror as an older, thin man in a shabby, nondescript work uniform jumped out from his driver's seat. Frozen within the gloom of our house, I observed the man open the back door of his van with a chilling nonchalance.

Out of the corner of my eye, I saw the cell phone. Sitting atop its stool like some absurd statuette. I could run to it, push 9-1-1 on its spongy keypad, and the police would be here in ten, maybe fifteen minutes. But what had the police done for us so far? The last time I saw a police officer, he was at my front door to arrest my mother. My parents had told me repeatedly to trust nobody, and at that point, "nobody" included the cops.

A flash of movement outside snapped me back to attention. When I saw the man sling a tool bag and orange extension cord over his shoulder and slam the van's back doors, a wave of adrenaline rushed up through my legs. I heard my father's voice in my head: *If someone crosses the gate, they're yours.* I had to defend the property from this intruder.

I was still in my pajamas, the ones with the pin-striped maroon pants and matching top. I went to the kitchen and quickly grabbed the biggest knife I could find, then slinked to the utility room, where I slipped my feet into Mom's stained barn shoes. I didn't think about being a young girl with a massive knife I had no idea how wield defensively. I only thought that I had to protect the property and myself, as Dad had instructed.

Staying close to the limestone exterior, I ducked behind forsythia bushes before darting behind the ash tree closest to the driveway. Peering out from behind peeling bark, I watched the man amble down the gravel driveway toward the barn doors. Quickly, I improvised a strategy: I would surprise him from behind.

"Hey! Who...ARE...you?!" I shouted as I jumped out from behind the tree, holding the knife up high in front of me with both hands trembling.

"I'm the plumber!" The guy spun around, so alarmed his hands were now in the air.

"Plumber? What plumber?" I screamed. "No one told me there was a plumber coming today! I don't believe you!"

"Leonard called me," he said, beginning to back away in the direction of the van. I felt more confident now, powerful almost, and followed him with the knife still extended.

"He would have told me that. Get the fuck outta here!" I screamed as the man turned and ran through the gate. Tossing his bag into the passenger seat, he had barely closed his door before peeling out from the shoulder. I waited until the van disappeared from sight before retreating into the backyard. Once inside I changed into the day's clothes and tried to calm down by playing with the cats. I felt every minute until my father walked in the front door. I rushed to him and told him everything I had done.

"I took care of it," I said.

"You did exactly what I told you to do," he said, without a hint of hesitation. I could tell he was proud. Later, when Grandpa came home, Dad and I accosted him.

"Did you call a plumber?" Dad asked. I stood behind him with my arms crossed like an angry parent.

"Yeah, that was Whitey!" my grandfather said, chuckling. "Got a backed-up something-or-other in the trailer. I asked him to come out and look at it."

"Why didn't you tell someone?" Dad yelled.

"I just saw him down at the Legion," Grandpa said, ignoring Dad's question. "He said some crazy little girl chased him away with a knife. I told him that crazy little girl is my granddaughter!" At this, even my father laughed.

Mom laughed, too, when she came home. As if chasing would-be intruders away at knifepoint was just a cute part of growing up, like a cracking voice or a puppy-dog crush.

Even if my father had been amused, he had first been pleased with me for taking charge of the situation. I held on tight to that feeling.

On the afternoon the power got shut off, I was angry, but not with Grandpa for being so trusting—my parents hadn't given him the full rundown of our identity theft; they were worried he might say something about it to the wrong person, or even, inadvertently, to the identity thief. Instead I was mad that our paranoia ran so deep it seemed to create canyons of silence between us and the people we should have been closest to. I was pissed off that I had scores of homework to do, and the house was too dark to do it in. I was furious that whoever was terrorizing us had found yet another way to cause us harm.

While Dad scolded Grandpa, I trudged to the three-season room off the back of our house. I heaved my backpack onto the white wire table and myself into one of its uncomfortable patio chairs. The bright blue-and-yellow floral cushions contrasted harshly with the bleak, brown landscape just beyond the glass. The sun was setting, casting a milky glow across the backyard.

Wrapped in my winter coat and using the last of the late-afternoon sunlight, I started my homework. When the day finally slipped beyond the horizon, I used a flashlight to see my math problems. We lived like pioneers for the next twenty-four hours, while Mom sequestered herself in the bedroom with the cell phone, making calls to straighten out this latest disruption. I was eating two-day old popcorn for dinner, reading by flashlight the next evening, when suddenly the whole house shook back to life. The furnace rumbled awake and the lamp in the living room lit up as if by its own volition.

TWELVE

At some point during the tumult of these years—the unexpected visitors, the flickering utilities, and the overwrought conversations—something happened that nobody seemed to notice. I stopped being a child. That didn't mean I was an adult, because I wasn't quite that. But I had become a full-fledged *person* whose universe should have been expanding outside the four walls of our home, outside of my mother and father. But instead, my world was collapsing, getting smaller all the time. My paranoia, my obsession with our identity theft, tightened like a belt around the perimeter of my thoughts. The number of family members I was allowed to speak to was dwindling, and talking on the phone to my friends was so expensive it was effectively impossible. I was scared and deeply lonely. I was exhausted.

One of my only ways to socialize, and to be out in the world, was through 4-H. Throughout high school, I showed everything from guinea hens to cats, often bringing home a pile of ribbons. I had some friends in 4-H, but because so much of our work was done sequestered on our own farms, these relationships remained tangential to my life, and never grew into the kind of close friendships, I can now see looking back, I desperately needed. Instead, I became more dependent on my kinship with the animals; like my father, I sought solace in their tacit acceptance, their steady routines. They provided a stark foil to the volatility of my human family.

It was an early spring evening when I announced to my father: "One day, I'm going to figure out who is doing this to us, and we won't have to live like this anymore." We were watching TV and I was lying on the Tang-colored carpet of our living room. It was the first time I said it aloud.

We were marooned. Physically and emotionally. At night we sat quarantined behind heavy drapes, and our dark house—now surrounded with a horse fence secured by padlocked gates at all times—sat poised in its fields like a bull's-eye. During the day we went to school and work, we did chores out back, and we pretended with the commitment of a method actor that everything was just fine. Under no circumstances was I to speak about the identity theft, or about what was really going on behind the scenes.

"The less people know about us, the better" was my mother's refrain. My father parroted it often.

This wasn't a completely new phenomenon. Mom had trained me from a young age to be ever at the ready to tell people at church or the store how many 4-H ribbons I had collected that year, or that I had been chosen for the academic team. In the years prior to the identity theft, when we still used to go to parties at their friends' houses, Mom would instruct me to "act like you belong here." Belonging somewhere in rural Indiana meant being a happy family with a pristine farm. And so the hayfields on the south side of the house were neatly manicured, and when mowing the grass became my responsibility, Dad used to walk me around the yard afterward to personally demonstrate all the spots I had missed. Our fruit trees were impeccably groomed. Even those padlocked gates were made of a beautiful red cedar.

Me in college with one of my beloved cats.

Of course, the inside of the house was a different story. It was embarrassingly outdated. Shades of oranges and reds and browns—the colors of dead leaves, I always thought—dominated the carpet and curtains. So little had been changed from when my grandmother had decorated it in the seventies—the same dusty tchotchkes, the same faded, flowery furniture remained. In fact, if one of my dead grandparents had gotten up from their graves and returned home, they would have struggled to find anything out of place. On holidays, when Mom would cry because she missed her parents so badly, Dad and I would look at each other, quietly wondering if preserving their house like a museum was helping my mother's persistent grief.

Even during the full onslaught of the crimes committed against us, I was coached to report how great everything was going. In the car on the way somewhere I would wonder, "What's the script?" Any deviations would result in a full dressing-down by Mom.

All of it was an elaborate illusion, a magic trick we never stopped perfecting. On the outside, our lives looked solid and well put together, but on the inside, everything was falling apart. Everything including me.

This obsession with appearances ran deep and began well before the identity theft. My mother had struggled with her weight as long as I could remember. Once, when I was in first or second grade, I came home crying because the kids at school had called me fat. Instead of comforting me, or telling me that I wasn't fat (and in fact, quite scrawny), she said that, unfortunately, there was little to be done about it. "Eventually you will be," she declared, "big like me." After years of watching my mom try diets and take Dexatrim and argue with my father over her eating habits, this proclamation terrified me. Moments later I was in the barn, searching until I found a spare length of baling twine. I lifted my shirt and tied the itchy rope around my stomach so hard my skin turned red. I promised myself I wouldn't take it off until it became too loose to wear. It was my very first diet.

A few years later, Mom suddenly reversed her no-makeup policy and began promoting it as staunchly as she had previously forbidden it.

"Are you wearing any makeup?" she would screech at me before school.

Usually I'd mumble something about wearing powder, hoping that would mollify her.

"You need foundation! You can't leave the house looking like that!"

"But I don't like wearing it," I'd protest, like I was eleven years old and we were fighting over my baptism dress.

"No one will be able to stand to look at you!" she'd yell. I began to think she was right. After all, I had been bullied about my appearance for years. I never could seem to get it right for anyone—not for Mom, not for the kids at school. Maybe everyone was just trying to help and I was being too sensitive.

But on the days I felt fed up, I'd tell her I'd just as soon not leave the house if it meant slathering on face paint. On my weaker days, I'd stare past my mother's shoulder as she braced me against the bathroom wall and colored my face to her liking.

If I could make it out of the house without her commenting on the flatness of my hair or the length of my bangs, it was a good day.

I couldn't understand why it mattered what I looked like on the outside if on the inside I felt so profoundly shitty.

My relationship with food was even more complicated than the one I was trying to navigate with my mother. What had started as an attempt to not be like her slowly became a complex system of martyrdom in her name. In the car going somewhere once, I asked if we could stop to get sandwiches for dinner, since the cupboards were empty. Mom sighed but agreed, saying she needed to cash a check if she was buying dinner. So we stopped at the bank and I waited in the truck. Ten minutes passed. Fifteen. Finally Mom reappeared with a scant amount of twenties and a cashier's check. I figured I'd hear the story when we got home but all I heard was a lot of cursing between my parents. I put the sandwiches in the refrigerator and got into bed.

That night in my diary I wrote: *I feel this is my fault for wanting something to eat.*

My parents were so cash-strapped during my high school years that at times the only items in the cupboard were bags of dried beans, cans of mixed nuts from Dollar General, and flour. Instead of asking for something else, I started to collect what I could find outside, like my father and I used to. I would walk back to the woods and pick the wild raspberries that grew along the creek bank. In the summer I lived on squash and tomatoes I pilfered from the garden, and fall meant limitless apples from our orchard. When Mom claimed she didn't have the two dollars a day for my lunches anymore, I took apples to school. Eventually, I stopped even doing that. I was hungry but I felt emboldened—I could live without asking my parents for a single thing, and I was thin, just like my mother wanted.

A few pages later my diary reads: *I keep losing weight.*

Many teenagers have food hang-ups and body-image issues. Lots of teenage girls don't get along with their mothers. If I had been allowed to invite a classmate to the house, or go to a sleepover, or stay up too late talking on the phone, or have dinner with a friend's family who actually ate dinner together, maybe I would have found some camaraderie; perhaps I could have found some comfort.

Every morning my mom took me to school and every afternoon Dad picked me up. They were like tag-teaming wardens overseeing my sentence. I was trapped—by my parents' expectations, by the identity thief, by the lies we told and the ones lived—but not eating gave me control and made me feel powerful, even when I knew I was not.

I kept losing weight.

THIRTEEN

I CAN IMAGINE THAT to the people sealed in their air-conditioned cars whizzing down US 27, past our limestone ranch, past our perfectly pruned apple orchard and that wine-colored cedar fence, seeing a young girl and her father baling hay in the purple twilight of July was quite charming. I'm sure it evoked some patriotic feeling or a quiet sentiment about family values and Midwestern sensibilities. Maybe they smiled, satisfied that a young person was learning an indelible craft instead of planted behind a TV. But the truth of the matter was that every moment I spent in that field was pure hell, and I hated it.

Baling hay is a nightmare. Especially with a utility tractor better suited for mowing the front yard than reaping crops from colossal fields. The work required three pieces of equipment, including the mower, the rake, and the baler (all acquired as bargains from a neighbor who was a New Holland dealer), and a lot of manual labor. Other helpers cycled in and out each summer—my grandfather, kids who worked at Dad's store, a cousin and his friend here or there—but I was my father's constant farmhand. I didn't get paid for my work, other than the privilege, Dad said, of getting to keep the donkeys I had been showing. It didn't feel like a fair trade.

We baled during each summer month, getting out in the field as soon as Dad got home from the store, and staying there until 1:00 or 2:00 a.m., or whenever the person driving the tractor submitted to their exhaustion. We didn't stop for dinner, and each day my dad transformed from a kindhearted father into a never-satisfied farmer. We could always do more, he said—get out earlier, stay out later. When we did come in, we were too tired to eat. We hacked up chaff, now black and swimming in mucus, as we fell into each night's deep well of sleep.

The worst part about baling hay was that every day in the field felt like a perpetual crisis. Rain clouds were always gathering to conspire against us. My father kept his eyes on the sky, yelling unwelcome updates about imminent storms that usually never came with the intensity he predicted, if they came at all. But if the hay got wet, then the hay got moldy. Moldy hay was worthless. So we'd rush it to the barn, heaving each fifty-pound block onto the hay elevator (another deal from the neighbor), and then head out to do it all over again, only faster this time. The grueling labor could have been an antidote to the constant anxiety of our daily lives but instead it was simply a supplement to it. I needed out.

I was surprised when Mom said I could get a part-time job. Maybe it was because she had also recently made a leap, becoming a full-time stockbroker at the Edward Jones in Albany, a twenty-minute commute away. Of course, there were stipulations. I had to stay in Portland and she would have final say over where I could work. When the manager at Burger King called me back, Mom approved—and convinced Dad to approve—only because her friend Harriett worked there and could watch over me.

Harriett had been a friend of Mom's as long as I could remember. They met back when Mom frequented craft shows, setting up a booth to sell her calligraphy. Harriett was a weaver; she made intricate pieces using wool, fur, feathers, and other textiles. Soon, they were renting vendor spaces together. Harriett was from Texas and had short black hair. Her skin was weathered and clung to the long bones of her arms. She was a decade or two older than Mom and took to calling herself Grandma Harriett when I was around. She acted like one, too. She and her husband, Gordon, the retired director of the county department of child and family services, used to take me to Pizza Hut every year around my birthday. They would buy me my own kid-sized pizza and insist that the staff parade around the table and sing "Happy Birthday." It was a nice break from the insularity of my real family.

I was sixteen when I started at Burger King. It wasn't a great job but it had its perks. For one, I was finally out of the dark confines of the house and I no longer had to spend my afternoons in a field sopping in sweat. And because Portland's restaurant scene was so limited, everyone came to eat at Burger King at least once in a while, so I got to see a lot of people I hadn't since the identity theft began in full force.

Cousins and uncles, old friends would swing through the drive-through. I'd recognize their voices in my headset and greet them excitedly—like the pickup window was my front door— these people we had closed ourselves off from for years now. I knew I should be careful about who I talked to, but I was so eager to rejoin the world.

"Axton!" they'd say. "When did you get so old?"

Reconnecting with estranged family members had its drawbacks. Because Portland is tiny, Grandma Betz found out I was working at Burger King and began to frequent my new work-place. For more than a decade I had seen Grandma Betz only when we'd pass her house—on the east side of town near the fairgrounds. She and her boyfriend, Jake, were usually sitting out on the front porch of her tiny brown cottage. Just sitting, never doing much. Dad usually glared silently and gave a half wave as we passed, and I'd wonder what it must be like to have a mother so cruel you couldn't even know her. I felt sorry for him.

But now I was dealing with the mean old woman and mostly I just felt sorry for myself. I started as a cashier at Burger King, and sometimes worked as a hostess, which was actually more about cleaning up people's trash than seating them. When Grandma and Jake—each occupying different stages of obesity—would waddle in the door, I'd cut the quickest angle to the kitchen to beg the manager to reassign me there. When that didn't work, I was forced to interact with them.

"Now, you need to come on down and see me," she would say, not lovingly. Dry, ashy curls covered her scalp like a fungus.

"You know, 27 runs both ways," I'd say, mustering all my teenage sarcasm.

Grandma and Jake would order and take their seats closest to the drink machine. Then they'd just watch me—watch me serve other customers, watch me wipe down tables—sometimes for hours, until my shift ended or a spot opened up in the kitchen.

Grandma wore special shoes for her neuropathy. I knew that inside of them she was missing a few toes. Nearly everyone in my dad's family had died from complications of diabetes, and Mom had told me that Grandma had long ago stopped taking her insulin. Everything about her was off-putting; her presence was like the smell that lingers days after a dinner of fried fish.

Still, I remained at Burger King, my kinky hair spilling out from under the teal cap, the tips of my black, nonskid sneakers curling with grease. I had become thoroughly enamored of having my own money and wasn't going to give that up for Grandma Betz or anybody.

In Portland, the only place to spend money was Walmart. I felt especially lucky that the Burger King was in the Walmart parking lot, making break-time errands most convenient. Soon it occurred to me that I could use my money to buy diet pills, like the ones Mom had gambled on for so many years. They didn't work for her but I had the discipline she lacked, I wagered. I scanned the supplement aisle until I found the generic version of Dexatrim. Then I skipped hurriedly across the parking lot and back behind my cash register.

On other days I bought junk food, piles of glorious and fatty junk food. Potato chips, Little Debbie cakes, SweeTarts, and always a bottle of Mountain Dew. When I got home I'd smuggle it inside and hide it in different places in my room. I'd put the SweeTarts under a stuffed animal and a bag of chips in my closet. I certainly never put anything in the common areas—that food was mine and I wasn't sharing it. Forever "fat" and "sugar" had been bad words in our house; they had been the impetus for my mother's misery and my father's frustration. And now I was flagrantly breaking the rules. It felt as good as starving myself had. Every once in a while, I'd devour a day's worth of calories in the quiet solitude of my bedroom, knowing that when I was done, I would make up for it with another round of abstention, a couple of the little white pills.

The diet pills made me shake and wrenched my eyes open as wide as a goldfish's. I began gnawing them in half or in quarters in an attempt to curb their side effects. The truth was that my heart pounded most days without the help of knockoff diet pills.

Around this time, I was sitting in animal science class after lunch when suddenly everything went haywire. Nausea erupted from my stomach and my mouth went dry. I felt like I was trying to breathe through a very heavy gauze. Without asking, I shuffled quickly out of the room, holding the skin below my ears with the tips of my fingers, trying to stabilize my vision. I watched the carpet disappear below my body all the way down the hall to the nurse's office.

"I have to go home!" I told the nurse before she even asked what was wrong. Suddenly I remembered when I had felt like this. Camp Crosley. The chapel. This was the same as that. When I began choking on my breath, the nurse called my mother.

I spent the next seventy-two hours rocking in Dad's red La-Z-Boy or standing barefoot on the back porch, letting the December cold numb my body. In the middle of the night, my mother sleepily fed me some Unisom, which didn't even quell my shaking. My parents were frustrated. How could I be fine one minute and then *like this* the next? I understood it less than they did.

On the third morning, I felt a modicum of relief. I got ready for school and gathered my books. When I opened the door to leave, it hit me again, as conspicuously as it did in animal science class.

"I can't!" I managed to yell to my mother before retreating to my bedroom.

The next day I made it to school. I marched directly from my mother's truck to the nurse's office and told her I needed to go home.

Mom took me to our family doctor. After listening to her

talk at length about my symptoms, the doctor suggested I might be having panic attacks and referred us to a psychiatrist in Anderson, near the outlet mall on I-69. There I was diagnosed with panic disorder. The psychiatrist was an older, sinewy man who spoke in whispers. During our hour-long session my mother talked incessantly, though never mentioning the identity theft, my pulling a knife on a stranger, the cop at the door, the stolen mail, the shut-off lights, or the cell phone on the barstool. At the end of our meeting, the psychiatrist suggested we come in for family counseling, all three of us. In a sequence of events I could have predicted, my father refused and that was the last time we talked about therapy.

I was out of school for a month but even from my bed maintained my 3.714 GPA. When I finally managed to rejoin my peers, I traversed the halls of Jay County High School three times a day for my hit of Xanax from the nurse, sometimes taking all three before lunch. As for the diet pills, I kept them in a tin on my bookshelf at home.

FOURTEEN

We had just finished breakfast. Dad had assembled a plate for me of buttered toast, scrambled eggs, and fried spring vegetables from the garden. Normally I would have balked at the calories the meal contained but eating with my dad was too special an event to turn down. That he was off on a Saturday was even rarer. Soon he'd be out back for the day, and sitting quietly in the sun-soaked kitchen with him was as peaceful as I felt in our home in years. Mom had left before dawn for Fort Wayne; we had the drapes open wide. That was how we saw the car pull up.

It stopped for only a few seconds in front of the mailbox; Dad and I both watched. I felt my stomach—full of butter and eggs—drop like an anchor. What now?

Dad set down his mug; sunlight revealed the twirls of steam that rose from within it. The front door slammed. I studied the crumbs on my plate. The front door slammed again. I heard the La-Z-Boy yield to my father's weight.

"What wrong?" I asked as I entered the family room.

My father said nothing.

"Dad?" I said, trying to peer into his face, which was turned down like a darkened streetlight.

He said nothing.

Normally, when my father got upset, words did not evade him. Quiet by nature, he became deeply animated in anger. His silence on this morning was as menacing as the clinched-up envelope he held between his hands like a sword.

With an animal quickness, he stood up and in three strides had the cell phone in his hands. I heard ten tones and two rings. A lady's voice, muffled, answered the phone.

"I need to speak to Pam Betz, now," my father said in a voice I had never heard before.

It was the sixth or seventh Saturday Mom had spent in Fort Wayne. She had been making the hour-long drive each weekend to be mentored by another Edward Jones stockbroker on the finer points of recruiting clients and managing their assets. She had been struggling in her new role—something else she attributed to the backward town we were stuck in—and the long days up north were meant to bolster her performance.

"You need to get home RIGHT NOW." My father's voice ricocheted between the hard surfaces of the kitchen. Adrenaline worked at my jaw.

I knew it would take Mom at least an hour to get home. I padded quietly across the living room carpet and into my bedroom. I sat on the bed and tried to read. I played with Chunx, holding him like a baby and teasing his whiskers. I stared out from the crack in my drapes. At last, I heard the sound of Mom's truck pulling into the driveway. I moved to the door and stood, back against the doorjamb, bracing myself.

Dad must have greeted her at the front door.

"You want to tell me what this is?"

"I will if you give me a minute." I heard the sound of my mother's work bag hitting the floor and the swift transfer of the paperwork.

"This—okay, yeah—this is wrong, John."

"Oh, really? Tell me how."

"Look, I forgot to tell you that the mortgage company was acquired by another bank. That's why they are recalling the loan." Pages were being flipped. "So this must have been an administrative error—"

"They sent us a foreclosure notice in error?" my father said incredulously.

"You don't understand things like this, John. Don't try," she said in exasperation. Her voice moved to the middle of the room. "It's fine, I'll take care of it." Because Mom was the one with the college degree, the one who was once praised by professors for her natural gift with the principles of accounting, my parents had long ago carved their marital roles into stone: Mom was the expert with money; Dad was the person who gave it to her. No questions. No complaints. In theory, anyway.

"Pam, I'm pretty goddamned sick of this shit."

I flinched.

"You have no idea what you're talking about! You have no idea how much it costs to live, to buy things, to take care of this place! It's so easy for you—you just go out there and feed your donkeys and ride the tractor around, and I'm going out in this dump of a town trying to make us money, trying to pay to the bills. You can't even name our homeowners insurance, can you, John? Do you know how much your daughter's retainers cost us?"

"I give you all this money, Pam. Where the fuck does it go?"

I closed my door. This was venturing into familiar territory.

Soon they would be filing through their backlog of grievances like a Rolodex: Mom hated Portland and Dad's farming was the only reason they stayed. There was no money here, no jobs, no like-minded people. Dad couldn't believe how much Mom had changed. He said she was not the same woman he married, that she had become desperate and cruel. Mom accused Dad of always assuming the worst about her. Dad couldn't understand how we were habitually broke.

I drilled down into my trigonometry homework. I hated trig and I was becoming convinced it would be the reason I wouldn't go to college. I stared blankly at the meaningless signs and symbols on the page. The yelling continued.

Cosine, tangents—I heard the word "divorce" slip under my door like a poltergeist.

Arc, area—Mom was screaming about the "fucking farm."

I put my forehead down on the cool hump of chapter 21. I thought about when Grandpa's body was lying where I was now. I wished he were here.

I'm not sure I realized what I was doing before I did it. I stood up fast and flung my trigonometry book behind me across my room. My 4-H ribbons twisted and fluttered in its tailwind before it slammed against the plaster wall, creating an alarming depression. I rushed out of my bedroom and through the dark house. The only light shining was the chandelier over the kitchen table; it looked like an interrogation room. I struggled to see my parents, who had their hands clasped tightly around each other's collar. Mom was pressed against the yellow Formica counter and Dad was inches from her face with his back to me. They were growling at each other.

"Shut up!" I shrieked. "Just shut up!" I drew the last syllable out for effect. My parents both froze; I could tell my volume surprised them. They loosened their holds on each other, as if I had broken a spell they'd both been under. I jammed my body between theirs and ordered Dad to move across the room, by the popcorn popper where so many of my meals had come from lately.

"I can't even do my trig homework because you guys are in here screaming at each other. I don't know what your problem is, but I'm sick of it! If I don't pass this class, I won't graduate. And if I don't graduate, I'll never get out of this—this hellhole!"

Silent and embarrassed, Dad slumped into his La-Z-Boy in the family room and Mom collapsed onto the couch in the living room, weeping quietly. I went in the family room with Dad, wondering if this would finally be the end of it, the end of everything. I was breathing deeply like I was having an anxiety attack. I could hear the whoosh of blood in my ears.

Where we had only hours before enjoyed an unhurried meal, my father sat, staring at the floor.

"So what now? Are you guys getting divorced?" I asked.

"I don't know," he responded almost inaudibly.

I laughed and sighed at the same time.

I decided I'd try Mom. I found her in the living room, still sobbing.

"Are you guys getting divorced?" I said, toneless.

"If we get divorced," she said between heaves, "you'll have to go live with your dad because he has more money than I do." Her words struck me as melodramatic; her defiance had melted into an unfamiliar defeatism I had never witnessed from her. I stayed with her for a few minutes, and I tried in vain to calm her down by putting my hand on her shoulder. I gave up and returned to my homework.

* * *

When my parents came into my room holding hands sometime
around 11:00 p.m., I was furious, but not surprised.

"Everything is fine, sweetie," my mom said.

"How? How are we going keep the house?" I asked.

Dad was going to drain his 401(k) to save the farm and we
would all stay there—as a family—after all.

Such was our definition of "fine."

As I got older I began to suspect my father's desire for
a happy—or at least *intact*—marriage (something his parents
couldn't achieve) was the glue that held them together during
their worst moments. If my dad sometimes let this desire over-
ride rational thought, it was only because it had been etched so
deeply into him during those long nights of his childhood, lying
awake and fearing his mother's footsteps. If he forgave my mom
for so many mean words and mistakes, it was only because he
was so motivated by how he wanted things to be and so blind to
the way things really were.

But while I sat at my desk in my bedroom, after my parents'
weak apologies and reassurances, I didn't care about my dad's
passivity or my parents' ability to sweep massive problems under
a rug. I was still reeling from the emotional whiplash of their
ten-round argument. All I knew for certain was that I had
endured about all that I could of Mom and Dad's bullshit. I was
done with these fights, done with these earth-shattering pieces of
mail tied to and shoved under the door, done with having every
aspect of my life interrupted. I had to get out.

FIFTEEN

TO WHOEVER BROKE INTO my locker the following Monday, stealing the pretzels I had brought for lunch and slinging my folders down the hallway like a shufflepuck, I owe a deep debt of gratitude. Had this asshole decided to be decent human being that day, or to inflict this indignity on someone else's property, I would have been stuck in Portland, Indiana, for eight miserable months longer than necessary. But when grade cards were handed out in AP Biology later that morning, and I noted my fifty-nine completed credit hours next to the forty-six needed to graduate, I marched to my guidance counselor with a fresh rage still burning in my chest.

"Why am I still here?" I said, holding my grade card up like someone bidding at an auction.

He confirmed that I would be able to graduate as soon as I took senior English, government, and economics. I had just missed the FAFSA priority deadline, but he loaded me up with paper applications for different colleges anyway. He was confident, which in turn made me confident, that I would be leaving high school—and Portland—a semester early.

The only people left to convince were my parents.

Still tender and soft-spoken after their fiery battle, my parents were at first a unified front of *absolutely not*. I was too young to go to college. I had expected the resistance and wasn't deterred. I worked on Mom first. I lamented about the academics at Jay County High School, about the lackluster curriculum. The same tactics I used to get out of public school in eighth grade worked just as well this time around.

"But what about prom?" she asked. "What about walking with your class at graduation?"

I didn't tell her we couldn't afford a ticket to prom and that my relationship with my peers was, at best, an anthropological curiosity on my part. Instead I listed all the reasons I was so eager to begin my college education. When she gave in, I moved on to the much harder task of convincing my father.

"You can go, but your mom's driving you and I'm picking you up," he said after hours of debate at the kitchen table. He meant I could go to Ball State, in Muncie, forty-five minutes from the house. "You're not living on campus. It's too dangerous. I know how those kids are at Ball State—I've hired a lot of them at the store. We need you here, anyway."

"That's great, Dad, except I, um, I want to go to Purdue."

"Absolutely not. No. Not happening." He shook his head and got up from his chair.

"You know what? Fine!" I began, halting his walk to the back door. He turned to look at me.

"If I can't go to Purdue, then just get me a job at the store. I'm going to be just like you. I'm not going to college and I'm not going anywhere! Ever!"

My father, unimpressed, let the storm door swing open behind him.

* * *

A month later, we were touring the campus at Purdue. Brick, castle-like buildings framed a neat square of grass. So far my mother had been positive about the campus, but that wasn't a surprise. She was the one who had greased the wheels and convinced Dad to come to the prospective students' event. "Let's just see it," she had said.

The quad was abuzz that day, as employers from all over the state had come to recruit some of the best graduating engineers in the country. Students in suits swarmed the common area, moving with a quiet enthusiasm. I would learn the following year about this event, the Industrial Roundtable, it was called, but for now the well-dressed crowd seemed a bizarre phenomenon, and a serendipitous one as it turned out.

"I gotta tell you, Axton. I'm impressed by these kids," my dad said. "Did you see how well they were all dressed?" Hours later, as the sun set behind us on Highway 26, he gave me his blessing to enroll in classes, one semester early, at Purdue.

I didn't attempt to dispel my father's misperception. If he wanted to believe I was attending a university where the boys wore ties every day, so much the better.

What he didn't know, I reasoned, couldn't hurt him.

And I really believed it.

PART II

SIXTEEN

WEST LAFAYETTE, INDIANA, lies a hundred miles due west of Portland. The two cities both reside on the fortieth parallel, within just a few hundredths of a degree, and I often picture them on the road map of the state, a straight line and a finger's length apart.

In real life, the distance between these two places is immeasurable. Portland is, well, Portland—full of small farms and small minds. West Lafayette is home to one of the world's foremost research institutions. Its diverse population is well represented by the various worship centers around town and the ethnic restaurants that line State Street, Purdue's main thoroughfare. Buses and bikes are the primary mode of transportation in West Lafayette, and I'm not sure there's a donkey within city limits.

To me, the best thing about West Lafayette was that nobody knew who I was. Purdue's attendance soared well above thirty-five thousand students during my years there, and the city boasts roughly the same number of year-round residents. Here, I could disappear into the masses; I could be normal. I stopped worrying about someone hiding in the bushes, or the next bad thing that was going to happen. I started worrying about gloriously innocuous things like making sure no one stole my laundry and getting used to the communal showers. I still spent several hours on homework each day, but it was quiet and I was uninterrupted by yelling or ominous knocks on the door. The only thing about home that I missed were my cats.

Because I started school in January, there was no freshman orientation, no silly welcome-week shenanigans to ease me into life on campus. That was fine with me. I came to Purdue feeling like an imposter. Everything I did was informed by the idea that the school did not need me but that I desperately needed it. This was my chance and I knew it. I declared a major in agricultural communications. My years in 4-H had instilled in me a deep love for animals and I had always liked to write; winning the young authors' competitions in elementary school had always been a point of pride. I imagined myself on staff at *Farm World* or *Hoosier Farmer*, writing articles about caring for a sick herd or new designs in chicken coops. At eighteen this felt like an enormous aspiration, and I was ready to work tirelessly to make it come true.

That meant many afternoons and nights behind the desk in my dorm room, skipping lunch or dinner or both. The hollow feeling in my stomach made me feel strong, and the less food I ate, the less money I'd have to ask for from my parents or borrow from the government. If living off vending machine pretzels and a daily salad from the cafeteria meant I'd be spared from the burden of debt, I was ready to make that sacrifice.

I lived in Windsor Hall, an all-female dorm in a stately brick building that looked more like a castle than a residence hall. My room looked like all the others—stark white, crowded with generic wooden furniture. The thing I remember the most about those first few months of freedom was one small but poignant detail—the phone in my dorm room. Sometimes I would stop whatever I was doing to walk over to my roommate's desk. I'd stand above it for a beat before picking up the black receiver. Holding it up to my ear I would sigh deeply, listening to the simple, steady sound of the dial tone.

* * *

One hundred miles east on the fortieth parallel, Mom and Dad were going through some big changes, too. Only a few months after I had left Portland for good, Mom's colleague Greg Reinhold was fired from Edward Jones for embezzling almost $300,000 from an elderly woman and her son. Dad had never liked Greg but Mom counted him as a close friend. She was especially torn up about it because she said she had been the one to blow the whistle. She said that Greg's secretary had asked her to look over what she thought were questionable transactions. My mother wasn't the savviest stockbroker but she said she knew what Greg was doing—investing his client's money in his own business—was highly unethical and very illegal. She said she had no choice but to report the fraud. The story ran on the Indianapolis TV news affiliates and in the *Indianapolis Star*. Because people had known Mom and Greg had been close, her already small client base began to thin. It wasn't long before she, too, was officially let go from Edward Jones.

More than anything, it was a knock to her ego. She had liked calling herself a stockbroker, reveled in seeing her face on the billboard by the veterinary clinic outside of Albany. If the job had been all-consuming and high-stakes, the boost in her self-confidence had been its redeeming ballast. She began immediately to look for other jobs, but her name had been—unfairly or not—tarnished, and months went by with no callbacks.

With little to do but job hunt and fret about finances, Mom

reignited her campaign to get Dad to sell the farm. I joked that it took her twenty years to convince him to move ten miles, but it's one of those things that's only kind of funny because it's entirely true. She wanted out of that house and away from the "money pit" it had become, she said. The foreclosure and my tuition hadn't helped things. Mom swayed Dad with the idea of a new life, unburdened by the past and wide-open with possibility. And she knew just the place she wanted to go.

The little white farmhouse south of Redkey spoke to her. She had passed by it for years, many times during the week, and most Sundays on her way to Dunkirk for Mass. It was less formidable than the limestone ranch in Portland, downright inviting with its wraparound porch. She knew Dad would be enamored of the massive red barn next to the house, and there was plenty of field for his animals to graze. Best of all, it was less than a tenth the size of their current land and therefore much cheaper.

Dad on the wraparound porch of the house in Redkey,
with his American bulldog, Maverick.

Whether Dad submitted to the new plan out of excitement or exhaustion didn't matter too much to Mom, and I was summoned from school one weekend to help them purge the old house. It had been months since I was home, but in many ways it felt much longer. As I drove down the country roads I had grown up on, I couldn't believe how foreign it all felt to me now.

"Was it always this dark out here?" I asked my mom that night, returning to my childhood home for the last time.

She laughed. "You've been away so long, you've forgotten what dark really is."

So used to the anonymity of the city, I felt a bizarre tinge of déjà vu when I overheard Dad chastise Mom for writing "moving sale" on the sign she posted by the highway.

"Do we really want people to know that we're moving? Should we be advertising that?" he asked nervously. What would have struck me as a normal question a mere six months earlier now just seemed absurd. Apparently we were just supposed to disappear—from the house that had been in our family for the better part of a century—wordlessly and without a trace.

The yard sale had to have been one of Jay County's largest. Fifty years' worth of stuff—Mom's and Grandma Elliott's—was piled high along each side of the driveway. With little time and even less energy to price thousands of individual items, Dad brought home apple boxes from the store and charged five bucks for everything that would fit into one of them.

I noticed a change in my mother that day. With each apple box that was hauled away, she seemed a little lighter, as if she personally had been bearing the weight of those things for many years. She wanted a fresh start, and, from what I could tell, she was getting one.

Not only did she delight in the new house—insisting I come

home for every holiday I could to witness her over-the-top decorations—she also found a new job that ignited a youthfulness I had never seen in her. Dad had groaned about the three-thousand-dollar headhunter she had hired with money taken, yet again, from his 401(k), but in the end Mom's gamble paid off when she was hired as a sales and promotions coordinator at Q95 in Indianapolis. The radio station was the most listened to in the city and famous nationwide as the home of Bob & Tom, the original irreverent morning talk show. Suddenly, instead of making small talk at Jinny's Café, Mom was hobnobbing with famous musicians and comedians, including Ron White and John Mellencamp. Her actual job sounded like a farce. It was her responsibility to plan events like pancake-eating contests and stripper boxing events.

She began dressing differently. Throughout my childhood she had spent considerable time and money trying to change or cover up a body she felt ashamed of. But when she took the job at Q95, she began wearing short skirts and tight, low-cut tops that showed off her curves. She was at last comfortable with herself, it seemed, and satisfied with her job. "I'm working with a different caliber of people down there," she told me.

She was hanging out with a different crowd, too. Most of her friendships had withered in the wake of the identity theft, but with the new house and new job came a flood of new friends. More and more when I called the house, Dad picked up and said Mom wasn't there. She was out with her friends at the diner, he would tell me. Some of the names I had heard before—Maxine was an old pal from her Edward Jones days—but the others were strangers to me, and even to him. We didn't express it to each other, but we were both happy Mom was socializing; what was good for her was good for us.

My parents kept the blinds in their new living room open. During my first couple of semesters at college I rarely asked about the identity theft, and it appeared as though my parents were finally moving past the financial carnage of my teenage years. Maybe we had made it through to the other side, I thought. Maybe all that was finally behind us.

SEVENTEEN

I KNEW WHAT THE salmon-colored envelope meant. Green envelopes were for bills but the dirty-pink ones were for encumbrance notices. I felt an angry heat travel up the back of my neck.

My mailbox was in the basement of my dorm. Nothing great ever came in the mail but I checked it dutifully. It was a small thrill to see my name on mail again, but my main motivation for trudging down the stairs every few days was staying on top of my tuition payments. After scholarships and grants, we owed a few thousand dollars each semester. Being a student at Purdue was the best thing that had ever happened to me, and I monitored my status—my grades, my financial aid—with the laser focus of an air traffic controller. Part of me now wonders if my diligence was leftover paranoia or some inexplicable premonition of things to come.

I marched upstairs, back to my third-floor dorm room, and dialed the four-digit code for the bursar's office.

"Miss Betz, I'm showing you still have the $2,534 balance here—"

"That's impossible; my mom took care of this," I said, making no attempt to disguise my rage. "This is a mistake."

"I don't know what to tell you." The voice on the other end of the line was indifferent, tired.

I hung up the phone and slipped on a pair of tennis shoes. The bursar's office was a short walk across campus and my fury would keep me warm enough to forgo a coat.

No one was very nice at the bursar's office, and I guess that stands to reason. I'm sure most of their visitors were a lot like me—mad, slightly panicked, perhaps a little irrational. There were, after all, bars separating the ladies behind the counter from the ne'er-do-wells on the other side. The walls of the office were a dingy gray; outside, naked trees shivered in the February chill.

"I just called. You said I owe money but I *know* my mom sent the check. Can you please double-check to see if you received it?"

"Miss Betz, I presume?" She was an older lady, wearing an oversized sweatshirt.

I perched my fingertips on the cold countertop while she shuffled into the back room. This woman had no idea how important this was. I could almost hear the second hand of the clock inching closer to the moment when I would be dropped from my classes for nonpayment.

Suddenly she reappeared with a check in her hand. My relief was halted when I saw it was stapled to a pink piece of paper. How exhausted I was with pink sheets of paper. "Go down the hall and to the right, please," she said.

As I stepped into a hidden side office, the lady closed the door behind me. The space looked like a small conference room, a windowless space for serious conversations.

"So. You were right; your mom did send a check." She let the words hover between us for a moment; I felt a punch line coming. "And it bounced."

But I had not expected that punch line. My heart made a familiar somersault. She stared at me, waiting for some kind of explanation.

"Look." I used a softer tone, realizing now what this woman thought of me. "My family has been dealing with identity theft for years. This probably has something to do with that. My mother would never write a bad check. Is there any way you could give me a copy of it?"

Without a word, she led me back to her desk, where I was now in front of the bars I had moments ago peered through. How different it looked from the other side. There was a very large soda next to her keyboard, and some pictures of kids I assumed to be her grandchildren; it was strange to see clues of this woman's existence outside this dismal office. She handed me the check.

It was my mother's check—same name, address, and bank. But it was not her handwriting. It was shaky and tilted in all the wrong ways. I stared at it long and hard, trying to figure out who wrote it, racking my brain to recognize the impostor's handwriting.

And just like that, I was a financial deadbeat once more.

* * *

My parents often visited on Tuesdays, because that's the day Dad usually had off work. They would make the two-hour journey from Redkey, arriving at my dorm midmorning. Typically we'd go to the grocery, and then go out to lunch, where I'd push a salad around a plate for an hour, fielding questions about my classes and dorm mates. They might hang out with me for a little while in my room, Mom practically glowing with pride and

Dad visibly uncomfortable to be surrounded by so many young women, many of them in bathrobes or pajamas.

I had purposefully waited to bring up the matter of the check until their visit a few days later. I was not going to let Mom blow this off like she did with so many other things.

"What is this?" I asked bluntly, pushing the check under Mom's gaze at my desk. Dad moved quickly across the room to see what I had given her. He leaned over the back of her chair while they both studied it.

"Hmm," Mom said.

"It's your check, your bank, your everything. Who would do this? Who would write a bad check for my tuition?" I walked up next to her with my hands on my hips.

"It looks like someone was purposely trying to disguise their handwriting," Dad said.

"I think so, too. Why would someone do this to me?"

"This is unbelievable, Pam." Dad's volume was inching up. "How did someone get your checks?"

"Someone must have mirrored my checking account," she said.

"Why would someone do that?" I asked again.

"To launder money. And to avoid detection, they steal mail and run legitimate-looking bills through the account before laundering money," she explained.

It didn't quite make sense to me, but visions of mobsters in dark, smoke-filled rooms came to mind. Bad men practicing my mother's name, her handwriting. By the look on Dad's face, he was conjuring similar thoughts.

"Okay, you two need to calm down. I don't know why you take the identity theft so *personally*. It's not personal." She got up with the phony check still in her hands, like she was protecting us from a dead animal, an obscene portrait, something we shouldn't look at.

"But it is, Mom. This is my education! It's very personal!" I was not going to let her invalidate my anger. "They're going to drop me from my classes if we can't pay this by the end of the week."

"Jesus, Pam. Who is doing this? This has gone to another level. We need to talk to someone about this."

Mom didn't answer. All three of us knew there was no one to talk to about this. No one to help us or tell us what to do. We were alone in this together.

Suddenly I knew how my father had felt for all those years, trying to get Mom to recognize how egregious this all was, or to convince her that something had to be done. Because somehow, after every conversation in which you were determined to call her to task, instead of feeling emboldened, you simply felt silly. Silly for taking things so seriously, silly for thinking there was anything to be done at all. I knew that she didn't want us to feel upset, but sometimes I wished she would just get upset, too.

A few days later, my payment posted mere hours before I was unenrolled from school. Dad sold off a couple of his donkeys to make sure I could stay at Purdue. I checked my mailbox every day until I received the receipt, tucked inside a pristine white envelope.

EIGHTEEN

THE APARTMENTS AT THE corner of Salisbury and Robinson were nothing fancy. Short brick buildings lined parking lots full of college-kid cars: mostly old beaters, some hand-me-down Beamers. I had taken the city bus across town to check out a studio I saw advertised for a sublet over the summer. As I walked up to number 63, the door to 62 swung open like a sudden gust of wind.

"Jorie?"

"Axton!"

"Do you live here?"

Jorie was a tough girl from the south side of Chicago. She had been kicked out of the dorm right after Christmas break for allegedly firing up a hibachi grill in her room. When the RA on our floor interrogated her about it, Jorie had apparently shrugged and said she had been told to be more social. I liked Jorie.

"Yeah—right here." She pointed to the brass numbers on her door. "Do *you?*"

"I'm hoping. I'm looking at this sublet today."

"Oh, I'm subletting my apartment this summer, too! You should just live in mine. You can use all my furniture and dishes and whatever you want." Jorie pointed. "How much is she charging?"

"Three-eighty."

"I'll do three hundred," she said.

So I subleased Jorie's apartment for the summer after my third semester. Finally out of the dorm, I reveled in the privacy and solitude of her dark studio apartment. The artificial comfort of the window unit was like a prayer rock, reminding me to give thanks every day that I was not baling hay.

I did get a familiar job that summer, though. I also learned that if you walk into just about any Marsh grocery store in the state of Indiana and mention the name John Betz, someone was probably going to hand you an apron and tell you to get to work. My days were busy—school in the morning, work in the afternoon—but I was the happiest I had ever been. When I noticed cats in one of my neighbors' windows, I decided to sign a lease on another studio as soon as Jorie came back.

It turned out that the apartment next door opened up in mid-August and so I moved my things a few feet down the sidewalk from Jorie's to my new place a few days before school started. I didn't have a lot, but soon I would have Chunx and Sunny. Mom and Dad came over on a Tuesday with the cats and a bunch of hand-me-down furniture.

A few days after I moved in, I received a letter from the electric company. When I had called to transfer service into my name, the company representative had moved through the process robotically, confirming the date and time I needed the lights to come on. I hadn't thought of it since. But now this letter was informing me that, because of my credit score, I would need to put down a deposit of one hundred dollars to maintain service. As a near-minimum wage earner, this wasn't great news, but I understood. I figured that, at nineteen, I probably didn't even have much credit.

I noticed a number at the bottom of the letter that I could call to request my credit report. I had never seen a credit report before—let alone mine—so out of curiosity I decided to make the call.

* * *

It had been a long day at school and the roots of a headache had planted themselves near the outer corners of my eyes. There were hours of homework in my immediate future but as I walked through the parking lot of my building, I wistfully considered a nap. The manila envelope I found folded over and jammed in my mailbox was the last thing I wanted to deal with.

With a groan of resignation, I yanked it from the box. It was a lot bigger than I had expected a credit report to be. *Must come with a lot of instructions*, I thought. Most of me wanted to drop it by the front door and forget about it for a while, but I leaned against the arm of my hand-me-down, green-floral-print couch with my legs crossed and tore it open instead.

There have been a few moments in my life when reality has skipped in front of me like a broken television—and I remember this one in slow motion. Sliding my finger under the thick flap of that envelope, feeling the adhesive give way and the paper tear in jagged intervals—those were the last indelible sensations of an existence I understood. And then, as sure as the sharp edges of paper in my hands, another existence took its place. A new life, a different identity.

I did not find any instructions inside the envelope. Instead, I found the report, with the bulk of a term paper, full of fraudulent credit card charges and collection agency entries in my name. Discover, Bank One, First USA. Pages of numbers and dates as foreign as a language I did not speak. The first line of credit had been opened in 1993, when I was eleven. That was the year my parents' identities had been stolen.

My credit score was 380. For a merciful second I thought maybe that was good. After all, 100 is perfect. It always had been in school, anyway. Then I saw the corresponding key. My score of 380 placed me in the second percentile of all scorers in the United States. About as low as it gets.

As my body folded over the arm of the couch, my mind struggled to make sense of these bizarre numbers. *Surely they'll know—I was just a kid; I couldn't have done this.* I felt the sting of tears on my cheeks. *Who would do this to me?*

I called Mom on the new cell phone she had bought recently, finally retiring the behemoth from its stool in the kitchen.

"I'll never own anything!" I sobbed. "A car, a house."

"Axton, this will get cleared up." She was driving home from Indianapolis, and I could hear the growl of I-69 under her Park Avenue.

"Mom, who would do this to me? And why?"

"No one is doing anything *to* you, Axton; they just got your information and used it. It's not a personal attack."

"It definitely feels like one, Mom."

Dad's reaction nearly broke the receiver. "This is a vendetta! This is someone with an axe to grind." I could picture him in the tiny back office of the grocery store, clipboards hanging on nails all around him. "If I find out who it is, I'm gonna kill the son of a bitch."

I didn't want Dad to kill anyone, but his response certainly felt more appropriate than Mom's. Either way, there was little either one of them could do for me. I had watched for years as they struggled as mightily and futilely as a fish on a hook, never quite able to regain the control of their lives that had disappeared with the donkey magazines.

I had so stupidly thought that I had extricated my life from theirs. That I would be able to witness their plight—with sympathy, of course—from a distance, safe in my quaint college town with my good grades and two beloved cats. Checks could bounce, but ultimately I would be fine because *I* was in control of my own destiny. It wasn't the first time my naivete was exposed, and it certainly wouldn't be the last.

NINETEEN

IDENTITY THEFT BECAME A federal crime in 1998 with the passage of the Identity Theft and Assumption Deterrence Act, but its impact was largely rhetorical. Prior to this legislation, identity theft was considered an offense against the financial institutions that were losing revenue due to unpaid charges. Little to no legal consideration was given to the people whose lives were destroyed by the fraud committed in their names. The act changed that. Although it didn't do much to assist law enforcement in apprehending these criminals, it did establish baseline jail time and fines for the perpetrators of identity theft, when they could be found. It also provided the affected with a loaded but handy new moniker: *victim*.

I hated feeling like a victim. My parents were victims; I did not want to be one. I wanted to be a fighter. To take back my credit, my identity, the things that were mine.

Sitting on a folding chair in front of my Compaq desktop computer, I typed "identity theft help" into the search bar. One of the first results was a semirecent MSN article about how to report the crime to the authorities. I nodded heartily as I read that local police were often hamstrung by a lack of resources and the inability to prosecute across jurisdictions. Mom had said she had been working with the Jay County police for years—but so many of the crimes committed against us happened outside of the county. Maybe it made sense that little progress had been made in our case.

I felt confident—too confident, in hindsight—as I drove to the state police post in Battle Ground to report my identity theft. These troopers had jurisdiction over the whole state, and the crimes happened within the state, so surely they could help me. Visions of car chases and gunfire swirled through my head like a carousel.

I maneuvered my '88 Park Avenue expertly—thanks to the tractors I had grown up driving—down a winding Highway 43 on the way to police post.

Battle Ground is a tiny town so named for the Battle of Tippecanoe, an important fight during the Indian Wars. Then Governor William Henry Harrison marched a thousand of his men to Battle Ground, where they set up camp on a ridge above the Indian stronghold. Fearing a surprise attack, Harrison instructed his men to sleep in battle formation, fully clothed. Sure enough, Tecumseh's men laid siege around 4:00 a.m. Harrison's soldiers were ready. After a bloody fight, they claimed a decisive victory, celebrating by burning the Indian village to the ground and destroying any winter rations they had found along with it.

Driving into Battle Ground that day, I half expected to find evidence of this brutal history, some kind of scar on the land that might indicate how many people's lives had ended here. Instead, the most dramatic thing I found was the foliage, fiery red against an autumn morning. The town itself was just a collection of two-story buildings crumbling near a railroad track; the police building was even less impressive. It looked like a gray shoebox with an American flag planted out front.

Holding my credit report like it was a speech I was about to deliver, I walked inside. Once again, I was separated by a glass partition from the police officer manning the front desk. Besides this sole employee, the building felt empty.

"Can I help you, miss?" The officer looked up from his paperwork.

"Hi, yes. My name is Axton Betz, and somebody stole my identity."

The officer looked at me expectantly.

"This is my credit report." I slid the papers under the glass. "I didn't open any of those credit cards. And I didn't use them to buy anything."

The officer looked at the report, and then at me, and then back at the report. He didn't ask any questions, just quietly flipped through its pages. Then he began to type notes into his computer, copying my name and address from the front of the report. After about two or three minutes of silence, he pushed my materials back through the slot, along with a piece of paper that bore a circled case number and the following sentence: "Unknown suspect opened credit cards in victim's name."

That was it.

"Show this to the creditors, and good luck, Miss Betz," he said, his eyes returning to the screen in front of him. That was the beginning and end of police involvement in my case.

On my way home, I glanced at the gentle hills that rise over the Wabash River, where Harrison and his men had sat patiently. I thought about them up there in the dark, with their eyes wide open and their guns ready, waiting on an attack they

knew would come. I thought about the ways in which my childhood had been like that night—the paranoia, the watchfulness.
A lot of good it had done me.

* * *

I should have known better than to expect someone to help.
When had anybody helped my family during the many years of
our crisis? I pushed despair away like an unappetizing meal. I
would not give up.

I studied the credit report for what felt like the hundredth
time. My online research had informed me that First USA
had been acquired by a financial conglomerate. But Discover
Card had a number I could call. Once again armed with my
credit report—and now a police case number—I dialed the ten
numbers intending to clear my name.

"Those charges were not made by me. I was only thirteen
when the card was opened."

"I'm not sure how you expect me to believe that, Miss Betz."

"I can give you a case number. This is an incidence of
identity theft."

"In cases of identity theft, the perpetrator opens a card, maxes
it out, and walks away. Somebody made two payments on this
card and then simply stopped. How do you explain that?"

I did not know how to explain that.

"I don't know, but it wasn't me." I was suddenly aware of how
young my voice sounded on the phone, how incredible this all
must seem to a stranger.

As I worked to repair my credit—often in vain—I learned
just how difficult it can be for a person living in debt, let alone
debt that isn't theirs, to simply exist in the world. I became prey.

My mailbox was suddenly overflowing with thick envelopes from collection agencies, from attorneys attempting to collect debts that were not mine. The cheap plastic phone by the refrigerator rang a dozen times a day. Once, it got so bad I paid the phone company to change my number. Things were gloriously quiet for a few weeks until the collection agencies tracked me down again.

Collection agencies buy debt from credit card companies, and other types of financial lenders, for cents on the dollar. Their gamble pays off only if they are able to reclaim the lost money (and then it can pay off to the tune of tens of thousands of dollars). But in order to squeeze that money out of people who likely don't have it, they resort to some pretty ugly, and often illegal, tactics. I've had debt collectors threaten to call my neighbors or my employer in an attempt to shame me into coughing up the cash (this is illegal). Debt collectors have threatened to garnish my wages (not illegal, but impossible without a court order). It is not uncommon for debt collectors to ask to speak with family or friends, so that they can explain the situation and suggest lending their loved one the money. Some even convince the debtor to send a postdated check in an attempt to seize sensitive account and routing information.

Recalling the phoneless house of my teenage years, I began to realize how especially damning it had been to lose that connection to the outside world. Not only could we not call out, but no one could call us—even if they were creditors—if for nothing else than to alert us to the charges being made in our names. I was starting to see how calculated this whole thing was. It was difficult not to feel outmatched and outsmarted.

But I pressed on. I refused to pay debt that I hadn't incurred. Mom told me to not open the collection letters, to write *return to sender: addressee unknown* on the envelopes. I became immune to the terrible bleat of the phone. Whoever had stolen my identity had no idea who they were messing with, I thought. I had dreams of dragging them into the police post, or Discover Card's corporate office.

"This is the asshole who stole my identity—this is the piece of shit," I'd say. "Now do you believe me?"

TWENTY

AS IF SOMEONE OR SOMETHING was chasing me, I finished college at warp speed. I rarely went home during academic breaks and wedged as many classes into any term I could. With graduation around the corner, I began to consider what was next for me.

Two things happened that made me think twice about leaving the collegiate cocoon I felt so safe within. First, the economy tanked. My classmates—the lucky ones, anyway— were forced to take jobs selling seed corn on commission. I did not want to sell seed corn, and working in the private sector just didn't appeal to me. I wanted to affect people's lives, not just a few people's bank accounts. A position in an extension office seemed like a good fit, but I would need a master's for that kind of work.

The other thing that happened was that I got the opportunity to teach. In my honors psychology class, each of us was assigned to lead recitations for non-honors students. While most of my peers seemed nervous about standing at the front of the room, I felt at ease. For a long time my intelligence (as well as my innate desire for control) had felt like a handicap. But on that day, those personality traits felt like the assets they were becoming. To teach college, though, would also require an advanced degree.

And so I never really settled on getting a master's; it just seemed to settle on me. I applied to the program that seemed like the most natural continuation of my undergraduate experience—agricultural economics. At Purdue, Ag Econ is a competitive sport; I did not make the team. It certainly didn't feel like it at the time, but the rejection was one of the best things that happened to me professionally. It gave me the time and impetus to explore other options, which is how I stumbled into the Consumer Sciences and Retailing program. All those half-helpful articles I had found online had given me an idea.

Like a prisoner who earns a law degree from behind bars, I would study identity theft while trying to save myself from its effects. If I couldn't get away from it, I would run toward it. Perhaps I would find the perpetrator somewhere along the way.

* * *

Despite my abysmal credit score and the legions of debt collectors after me, slowly I was starting to feel like a real adult. I had a degree. I had a car (albeit a junker). I lived in an apartment on the bus line. I bought my own toilet paper. And I had been accepted into the graduate program in Consumer Sciences and Retailing. The only thing missing—at least according to my mom—was a husband.

Personally, I was content cohabiting with Chunx and Sunny. They provided me with all the affection I needed. But Mom insisted that, at twenty-one, I was quite the old maid, that I wouldn't truly be a responsible adult until I was betrothed. Her own young marriage had instilled in her the kind of fulfillment I wouldn't understand until I got my hands around it, she said. I didn't mention that neither she nor my dad had seemed all that fulfilled for a long time.

But I worried she was right. I also worried that no one would even want to marry me. For so many years my mother had been telling me that I needed makeup to cover my face, straighter teeth, more voluminous hair. That I needed to watch what I ate, smile more, wear dresses. I was beginning to see that during my pivotal teenage years, Mom had projected all of her insecurities onto me, but that didn't make the impact of her words any less real. Who, I thought, would want to be with someone like me? I had dated here and there, and nothing serious ever came of it. Chunx and Sunny hadn't warmed up to any of the guys I brought home, and I took that as a sign.

Reluctantly, I set up a profile on Yahoo!'s dating site. Maybe I could get someone to fall for me over the internet, so that they could overlook my teeth or my clothes when we actually met in person. For the first couple of weeks, I half-heartedly carried on a few conversations with boys who all seemed like duds in one way or another. But eventually, I found myself thinking a lot about a guy named Rob. Rob lived over the river in Lafayette, and had sent me a few genuine and interested messages. He was not a dud. He was a graduate student, working on his PhD in chemical engineering. At first our online chats were casual exchanges about our family cats, but soon we were talking on the phone for hours at a time.

My apartment had been well lived in; nail holes from previous tenants peppered the walls and a faded yellow Formica dominated the kitchen. It hadn't been remodeled since it was built, sometime in the seventies. By this point I had my old phone from childhood, in the shape of a cat, on an end table next to the Halloween-colored couch that Mom gleefully gave me after purchasing new living room furniture for the house in Redkey. It was on this couch, lying with that novelty phone balanced on my ear, that my future husband and I got to know each other.

Or rather, I got to know Rob, but he would say that he didn't really get to know me. Later he would tell me that I engaged in our conversations as if I were filling out a questionnaire. One-word answers. Bare minimum context. Of course, he didn't know that the reason behind my caution was that I wasn't used to letting people get close to me. By necessity and at the urging of my parents, I had become a master of evasion. When someone asked about me, I instinctually assumed their intentions were malevolent. Though it was no longer a conscious reaction, I feared that if I shared too much of my life with someone, they would somehow use that knowledge against me. So when Rob asked me about my parents or my childhood, I had to stifle the urge to say: "What's it to you?" or something like it. It never crossed my mind that he was asking because he sincerely wanted to know.

That didn't mean I couldn't listen. Rob regaled me with stories about his friends and classmates in grad school, about the softball league they played in. I learned about Rob's family back in Missouri, his three siblings. They were all bright. One of his sisters was attending school on an athletic scholarship. His dad was an engineer. The picture he painted was of a normal, happy family, with no financial worries. I was anxious about what he would think when he found out about mine.

Two months after our marathon conversations began, we agreed to a first date. Rob offered to cook for me at his apartment. In the hours before the dinner, my nerves were as taut as a tightrope, but I was excited. I decided to wear jeans, since we were just staying in. I wore my curly hair down.

When I arrived at Rob's place, dinner was ready. I had long ago stopped eating in front of other people—another mechanism of control and my disordered eating—but for this occasion, I made an exception. The floor was vacuumed and everything was dusted. His apartment was small but tidy, and brimming with the aroma of thyme and oregano. He stood in a cramped kitchen that exaggerated his already large stature, wearing plaid knit shorts and a T-shirt. I don't remember what pleasantries we exchanged, but I am positive they were brief and shy.

Dinner—jambalaya—was served on Rob's brown plaid couch, which I was a little relieved to discover was even uglier and more uncomfortable than mine. Sitting down on the couch was like sinking into a hole, so I opted for the floor. We set our dishes on the coffee table in front of us as we both earnestly struggled for conversation topics. Rob's shelves were filled with engineering and sci-fi books, CDs, DVDs, and other artifacts from his life we could point to and talk about. Soon, we had segued back into our ongoing conversations about Rob's family, his social scene. Again, I was filled with worry as he described an ideal upbringing and a tight-knit family.

This feeling of otherness was one I was used to. In addition to the identity theft that marked me, I was also always vaguely aware that my backwoods, lower-middle-class upbringing was far from the norm. It followed me like a shadow. Throughout college I drove beat-up, high-mileage cars, first Mom's old '85 maroon Crown Victoria, then an '88 Buick Park Avenue. One of the most offensive was a beige '95 Oldsmobile Cutlass. Its muffler had rotted off and I didn't have the money to replace it. I thundered all over town in that thing before I was pulled over and told I was violating the noise ordinance.

"Are you aware you don't have a muffler?" the officer had asked me.

"Oh, I do," I said matter-of-factly. "It's in the trunk."

Normally, I was good at not letting this feeling get to me. I had grown up surrounded by simplicity and need; I had spent a lifetime pretending my family was just like everyone else's. But now, sitting on this couch, in front of a guy I liked—a guy who had just made me dinner from scratch (I only knew how to cook from a box)—I realized the stakes were higher than normal. I had to tell him.

"I'd really like a second date," he said when our bowls were empty and we had exhausted conversations about our favorite movies and grad school friends.

"Well," I said, "you might want to reconsider that."

As I began to tell Rob about my family, about our experience with identity theft, about how broke my parents were—how broke *I* was—he didn't flinch.

"That must have been difficult." He said this or some variation after each revelation, without indication of fear or disgust. *Everyone has a breaking point,* I thought. *I just haven't found his yet.*

I still routinely received court summonses because of unpaid bills for credit cards that I knew nothing about.

"Really? That's tough."

I'd been taught to be so wary of strangers that I'd chased a plumber with a knife when I was fourteen. We were estranged from our extended family, and suspected that some of them were behind the crimes committed against us.

"You've been through a lot."

I received multiple calls a day from collection agencies. These calls came in waves and would be so relentless that I usually took the phone off the hook. When I was in high school the police came to our house one night to arrest my mom for check deception. I hid in my bedroom closet while Dad convinced the deputy sheriff that it was a mistake and just another instance of our identity theft.

"You must have been scared."

As I formulated each sentence, I braced for Rob's shock or rejection. But if Rob was worried about the chaos a relationship with me might entail, he sure didn't let on.

"What has it been like trying to fix this?" he said, as if he was reading out of a manual called *The Perfect Responses for Bad News.*

I left Rob's apartment that night with a second date lined up and a chest full of relief. I couldn't believe I hadn't scared this guy off, because I had *really* tried to scare him off. I walked to my noisy old junker enjoying the vague flutter of butterflies in my stomach.

Soon we would be seeing each other every Friday and Saturday night and it wasn't long before we were an official couple. I never felt less-than in Rob's company, or worried about the way I acted or looked. Most importantly, though, Chunx and Sunny liked Rob. They danced between his ankles the first time he came over. That was all the reassurance I needed.

* * *

Of course, a relationship is so much bigger than the two people in it. A real, committed relationship means negotiating terms with the other person's family and lifestyle. It means sacrificing your time to support your partner. It means accepting another's baggage as your own. It means going to weddings together.

When Mom found out about Rob, and when she found out that I had been invited to his sister's wedding in Saint Louis, everything suddenly became about her. She dragged Dad across the state to take me shopping for an appropriate dress and shoes, as if I couldn't be trusted to pick out an outfit for myself. In a strip mall Fashion Bug, she foisted a black dress on me and chose black shoes with uncomfortable ankle straps, as if I was some kind of pathetic Cinderella character. I was appreciative of the money she spent, but felt embarrassed, belittled, and less excited than I had been before.

The wedding itself was beautiful. The couple radiated happiness. But I'd be lying if I said I had fun. Instead I was lost in a haze of self-pity. Who would ever pay for my wedding? I thought. How was I going to fit in with this family, who seemed so carefree and fortunate? When Rob's dad's cousin asked how many weddings I had attended that year, I said, "None—people in my family tend to get divorced, not married."

I was sitting alone, an untouched piece of cake in front of me, when Rob put his hands gently on my shoulders.

"Let's dance," he said with a smile.

TWENTY-ONE

By the next semester it was time to come up with a topic for my master's research project. I struggled to isolate a research question, a vein of scholarship in which I would contribute something new. Because there was so little work being done in the area of identity theft, my options seemed as wide-open as an Indiana soybean field.

If I was being honest with myself (and my committee), my persistent, resounding question was: *Who did this to me?* Of course, a topic like that would be biased, unscientific, and un-passable. So instead I chose to research people's attitudes about identity theft, the precautions they took, and if these thoughts and behaviors differed between urban and rural populations. It is glaringly obvious in hindsight how thinly veiled my own intentions were. How I had carefully, if subconsciously, chosen those particular constraints so that I could survey my own rural community, Portland, and perhaps somehow communicate to the identity thief that I wasn't giving up, that I was coming for them.

My assistantship didn't cover the printing and mailing costs associated with sending out surveys to participants. When I asked my mom for some money to help pay for the study, she balked, saying she and Dad had no extra funds that year.

"I'm probably sending one of these to the thief themselves, Mom," I told her proudly, undaunted by the out-of-pocket costs I was incurring.

"You're obsessed with this," she said flatly. At least Dad was enthusiastic about my research.

Working on this research helped to convince me that I wanted to pursue a PhD. There was so much more that needed to be learned about identity theft. While there were scraps of research available here and there, virtually nothing was being published on childhood identity theft. It was a void I knew I could fill...and, of course, a way to extend my surreptitious investigation for four more years. My advisor rightfully noted that to have any hope of getting into a decent doctoral program, I would need something besides "retail clerk" on my resume. So I began applying for far-flung positions in community building and organizational leadership, any work that might make me look like the kind of candidate who valued intrinsic rewards over financial security—de rigueur for a graduate student.

I landed an AmeriCorps job in volunteer development that meant I could defer my student loans for a while and make some money while I finished my research project. It also meant I would be trading my urban digs to return to a dusty, dying farm town like the one I was from.

The skyline of Havana, Illinois, consists of some rusty grain silos and a locally famous brick water tower. Once-ornate Victorian facades line a Main Street that at its terminus becomes a boat launch. Today an economically depressed area, Havana used to enjoy the nickname "Little Reno" for the gambling boats that crowded the banks of the Illinois River there. Al Capone was a regular in Havana, and the town was quite well-known for its legendary carousing. When I arrived, the most exciting thing about Havana was its new riverfront park. The place reminded me of my mother's dilapidated Shangri-la, Indian Lake.

My job was in city hall and I lived less than a block away in an old hospital building that had been converted to awkwardly sized apartments. A few weeks after I moved in, something unexpected came in the mail: a credit card offer. I was twenty-three and it was my first.

I was well aware that, along with somehow getting the fraudulent charges removed from my record, I needed to build some good credit to negate the bad. So far, I hadn't really gotten the chance. I jumped at the offer for a credit card, even though it was through a sketchy subprime company with an annual fee of $69, more than a fifth of its $300 credit limit. Even with the 29.99 percent APR, my new card was considered platinum. I shuddered to think what tragedy had befallen those who only qualified for gold, or, God help them, those who got the silver.

* * *

It was only a couple of weeks later when my car started sputtering and lurching like an old wooden roller coaster. It was a beater of a car and not worth repairing, but acquiring a new one—with my credit score—would be tough. I set out on foot for the two car dealerships in Havana. At both, I was told that I would need a cosigner.

"You don't understand; I don't have a cosigner. My parents have had identity theft happen to them worse than I have," I argued. It hadn't taken long for me to become weary of people's incredulity in response to my circumstances. The narrowing eyes, the skeptical head tilts. I tried to toe the middle line between demure and demanding, but what I really wanted to do was shake shoulders, get nose-to-nose, yell: "It's the truth!"

"Sorry, but you'll need a cosigner," said the two indistinguishable car salesmen I spoke with.

I walked back to the office with my head down, gritting my teeth with anger. My mind worked furiously to untangle yet another desperate quandary. I worried that without a car, I wouldn't be able to visit Rob, who had moved back to Saint Louis when I left West Lafayette for Illinois. He had been so supportive, encouraging me to follow my ambition even if it meant long drives and lonely nights for him. We were talking on the phone every day during our fledgling long-distance relationship, but I wanted to see him, and not just when he could swing a visit. By the time I was hunched over my desk again, I was still no closer to a solution.

City hall in Havana used to be a bank. It was a large room that was probably, at one time, quite stately. Large aerial photos adorned the walls; records were kept in the old vault behind my desk. But like most places in the small town, city hall desperately needed new carpet and a fresh coat of paint. There were about a half-dozen desks strewn haphazardly about the room, occupied by employees and volunteers. I would have preferred a more private space to get work done, but I appreciated the camaraderie, too.

Suddenly a set of keys splayed out with a surprising jangle on the desk calendar in front of me. I looked up to see the mayor— still dressed for his day job at the foundry, steel-toe boots and all—standing in front of me.

"What's going on?" I asked innocently. I knew full well what the gesture was, but I had been taught to never, under any circumstances, accept charity.

"I hear you need a car," he said, his gray eyebrows arched.

"I'll be fine," I said, forcing a smile, and pushed the keys back toward him.

"Take my keys and use my car to go car shopping this weekend." It was Thursday, which meant I was being offered a free car for four days.

"I can't. It wouldn't be right," I said, embarrassed and trying to discern if this was kindness or pity (neither sat particularly well with me), if I should be flattered or offended.

The mayor's secretary, a stout older woman, chimed in from the front of the large room: "I don't really see how you have much of a choice here."

I realized she had a point.

I set out on Saturday at 7:00 a.m. for Springfield, the state capital about an hour away. I paid extra attention to the speed limit and was vigilant to the point of absurdity, checking and re-checking the vehicle's unfamiliar blind spots. My list of problems was quite long already; I certainly didn't want to add to it by wrecking the mayor's car.

Springfield is a sizable town with a number of car dealerships. I spent about three hours driving from lot to lot, not even looking at cars until I asked a salesperson to check if they could sell to me.

"You'll need a cosigner," each one said eagerly, like my own personal chorus of disappointment.

I drove another half hour east to Decatur. The first dealership I visited was holding a tent sale. As a walked up to the tent, an enthusiastic salesman greeted me. Out of desperation or fatigue or both, I blurted: "If you can finance me, I will buy a car today."

The man looked at me with a combination of surprise and sympathy. He disappeared into the tent and emerged several minutes later to tell me, "We can finance you with special financing. We have specific cars for our customers that qualify for this financing." I knew enough about credit to know that "special financing" was not special in a good way, but this was progress.

Once, not long before I moved away from Portland, I hit a deer coming home from work around 10:30. Luckily, I wasn't too far outside city limits—there were still doors to knock on so I could find a phone to call home. By that time of night, Mom and Dad were already asleep and the cell phone rumbled away unheard on its stool in the kitchen. I cycled through phone numbers I knew by heart and eventually recruited somebody to go over and bang on the windows so that Mom and Dad could come pick me up.

Maybe it was because of this car accident, or maybe because I had learned to drive in a three-quarter-ton extended-cab GMC truck, but I had always been drawn to larger cars. They felt safe. When the salesman showed me a Crown Victoria available for special financing, I went for it.

The salesman led me into the tent to finalize the deal and informed me I would need a cosigner for income.

"Income only?" I confirmed.

The young man nodded. Despite the half-moons of sweat that were emerging from under his arms, I had a good mind to hug him.

On Sunday evening I attempted to return the car to the mayor, sharing the good news that I had secured reliable transportation, but couldn't pick it up until Tuesday. He told me to keep the car until Tuesday night "or whenever." Such was the Havana code of hospitality.

* * *

The first real road trip I took my car on was to Lincoln, to catch a train to Chicago for a work conference. It was one of those events held in a generic hotel ballroom: lots of stiff tablecloths and forgotten glasses of water. The day was full of team-building exercises and motivational speeches that were so boring I'd have rather been stocking grocery-store shelves.

That night in a suburban hotel room, I flipped through a Chicago phone book, looking for my cousin Michelle's name. She was a lot older than me; I hadn't seen her since Grandpa Elliott's funeral more than a dozen years ago. I called every Michelle Lothamer until her familiar voice answered the phone. "Oh my gosh, Axton!" she said, reminding me of all those Burger King drive-through reunions.

The next night at dinner I listened with horror as she told me why it had been so long since we had seen or heard from that side of the family.

"After the fifth or sixth return to sender, we just figured your mom didn't want anything to do with us anymore. So we gave up."

I began to explain the PO Boxes, the missing magazines, the disconnected phone line, waiting for Michelle to tilt her head in that dubious way I was used to, to squint at me in disbelief. When she did neither, I suggested we order another round.

TWENTY-TWO

AFTER THE FIRST FEW YEARS of identity theft, my parents stopped theorizing about who was behind it. Most of their energy went into the phone calls and appointments that were required to dispute charges, plead for help, and keep the lights on. At some point, the identity theft stopped being a phenomenon and instead became more like a personality trait, a thing that defined them both. They internalized the crisis in their own ways—Dad became withdrawn, throwing himself into his ever-expanding hayfields and donkey herd. Mom became a body full of denial, repeating that it wasn't personal, that it would end soon, as if saying those things would spare her from the emotional ravages of our victimization.

When I made identity theft the central theme of my scholarship, I realized that I, too, was choosing to absorb these experiences into something essential to who I was. After all, graduate students tend to identify themselves by their specializations. It was the first thing you asked and answered at any gathering: "What are you working on?" It was an irony not beyond me that while I resented the ways in which these crimes had shaped my life, I was now choosing to shape my life around them. Someone had manipulated the very real facets of what we as a society consider my identity—my social security number, my credit score, my *name*—and was now effectively molding the intangible aspects of who I was, what I cared about, and how I spent my days. Often I wondered what I would be doing if identity theft had not happened to my family, what I would be studying or what job I would have chosen. I was working all the time to fix the measurable impact of these crimes, but what could be done about the opportunity costs so immense they represented a completely alternate version of my life?

Mom and Dad, 2009.

Everything that we had lost and everything I missed out on might be worth it, just a little bit, I convinced myself, if I could figure out who did it. If the story ended with justice or some kind of redemption, then it wouldn't be a sad story anymore. Those opportunity costs wouldn't matter because the opportunity I got would trump all the others I could have had.

My research was progressing. I was learning about traits common to identity theft perpetrators. They were often impulsive; they made large or many purchases without the means to back them up. Often they were chemically dependent, or living second lives. With the pieces of information I was gathering—along with the remnants of Mom's conspiracy theories—I began keeping a list of suspects. An early draft looked eerily like a roster of people we might invite to my graduation party. If we still talked to people or had parties like that.

- My dad's brother, Harold. Harold and my dad didn't speak to each other and I had never met him. Mom said that he had a drug problem *and* worked for the postal service, which made him a prime suspect according to my research. Mom had suspected him, but Dad had blown it off. It had been more than twenty years since he spoke to his brother—why would he be trying to hurt us now?

- My dad's sister, Lisa. Dad and Lisa were close, after making it through their brutish upbringing together. Lisa got new cars on a regular basis. She and her husband went on frequent vacations. Mom often wondered out loud how they could afford it on their manufacturing salaries.

- The neighbors to the south of us, the Whitenacks. Mom called them the "carny outfit" since they seemed to make their living selling junk at flea markets. She said they looked like criminals. And once, I was in the room when she showed Dad a credit card statement for a fraudulent account. From what I discerned from their conversation, it had charges for gas stations all over western Ohio, from Indian Lake down to Cincinnati. There were a lot of flea markets that way, she insisted.

- My mom's friend Nila. When Nila and her husband built a horse barn, Mom was incredulous. "If Nila didn't work full time and her husband had a crappy factory job and spent a ton of money on booze, how could they afford a horse barn?" she wondered aloud. Also, Mom had long claimed Nila was "after Dad." Maybe, I thought, Nila stole Mom's identity because she wanted to *be* Mom. For a while, Nila had worked for Mom as a tax preparer; she would have had access to a trove of personal information, including ours.

- Mom's former and disgraced colleague Greg. Mom had said that Greg had been in charge of my parents' investment accounts at the same time he was embezzling money from his clients' brokerage accounts. When Greg got busted, Dad was adamant we had found our perp. Furthermore, Mom said she went to the bank to see about the tuition check that bounced and said the manager told her a woman with blond or light brown hair had been coming in and doing business under the name Pam Betz. Greg's wife had blond hair. Aunt Lisa had light hair, too.

I kept this list of suspects in a separate folder from my research; it was a personal project that I needed to keep away from the scholarship I was attempting. With everything I was learning, though, I returned again and again to the list.

But it was just a piece of paper. Scribbled with notes and names that, without the help of a private investigator or some kind of police involvement, didn't mean much. We had been cut off for so long from nearly everyone we knew, friends and family alike, that I couldn't very well waltz into their lives now and demand they answer incriminating questions. Some of the people on the list wouldn't even know who I was anymore, if they ever did at all.

So I never got the satisfaction of dragging a pencil across each name, as I methodically eliminated the suspects. And I definitely didn't experience the thrill of circling one of them with any kind of certainty that I had found the thief. Instead, the list only grew longer, until it took up the front and back of a piece of notebook paper. The helplessness and paranoia of my childhood loomed like a disease in remission.

TWENTY-THREE

When it was time to assemble PhD applications, I was less than excited. Just getting into a master's program had been a challenge, mostly because my GPA and GRE scores hovered around average. Although I knew a doctoral program was where I belonged, I braced myself for rejection letters—and the resignation that would have to come after. Lots of people spend their whole lives showing up to jobs that didn't fulfill them, I told myself. My own parents had done that. Maybe that's why I was so determined not to.

The job in Havana was eye-opening. Although AmeriCorps and the kindhearted people at the city hall meant well, my responsibilities—and my purpose—remained unclear for many months. It seemed no one knew why I was there or what I was supposed to be doing. Plus, the tedium and boredom of office work was getting to me. I hated sitting at a desk, staring at a clock. I longed to be back in the compelling confines of academia, but my application materials had been languishing for months on a bookshelf in my home office.

After one particularly crummy day at city hall, I came home

and walked directly from the front door to the computer, not even pausing to take off my coat. I knew I needed to use the deep dissatisfaction I was feeling to push through the fear of rejection. I was unsure of how I would pay for the application fees, but something had to change. I couldn't see myself doing the kind of work I was doing in Havana for the long term. In fact, I couldn't really see myself anywhere but back in a classroom—whether that meant sitting in one or standing at the front of it.

For some time, I had been considering Iowa State's program in Family and Consumer Sciences Education, because it was low-residency. That meant that if I couldn't get an assistantship, and have the tuition waived that way, I could find another job and work full-time and go to school piecemeal, paying out of my own pocket. I chose a few more schools as backups and quickly made out the checks to cover the application fees; I would have to skimp on groceries that month to cover them. That evening, as the setting sun cast an orange pall over the neighborhood, I walked across the street to the post office with a small handful of envelopes, half sure I was going to turn around without mailing them. But I did mail them, and a deep regret set in as soon as the lid slammed shut. Like a child, I kicked the blue box, wishing it would spit up the money I had just wasted. I was so convinced I wouldn't get in, I didn't even tell Rob I was applying.

* * *

It was still bitter cold the next time Rob visited me in Havana. The Illinois River floated by downtown in sharp chunks of ice. The baseboard heaters in my apartment left the air painfully dry. When Rob stepped inside, I threw my arms around him, feeling something solid and boxy in his coat pocket, pressing against my ribs. I pulled away with a smile. "What is *that?*" I said.

Rob had been staying with his family in Missouri for a few months while he figured out his next move. Part of that decision hinged on me, and since I didn't know where I was going, he didn't know, either. But we had talked about getting married. On the phone one night, Rob had asked what kind of engagement ring I might want. I answered something inexpensive, something simple; music to the ears of my underemployed boyfriend.

Rob left on his overcoat, suggesting we take a walk down by the river. I felt the tingle of anticipation as I put on my shoes. We walked hand in hand to the pedestrian bridge that spans Main Street, overlooking the river. It was freezing; downtown was empty.

Rob and I remember his proposal differently. I heard: "You haven't always been easy to be with," but he swears his preamble went more like "We've been through a lot of ups and downs." Either way, his knee landed on a wooden plank of the bridge as he pulled that solid, boxy thing from his front pocket.

"Axton, will you marry me?"

"Yes!" I shouted as I pulled him up for an embrace. The slow rush of the frozen river seemed amplified, the whole world abuzz for just us.

We celebrated at the Chuckwagon, Rob's favorite hole-in-the-wall diner in Havana. In the glow of our engagement, the waitresses were beautiful, the faded wallpaper downright regal.

After dinner I called home. Mom's excitement came through

with an unprecedented volume. "Oh, that's fantastic! That is such great news!" she said. I smiled as I admired the petite diamond adorning my finger. This was the happiest I could remember ever making her. So what came next was unexpected.

"I don't think you guys should have a wedding," she said. "Don't waste the money. You should elope!" Her tone had not changed but suddenly my high spirits plummeted.

"Wait, what? Why not?" I pushed the diamond around my ring finger with my thumb, until the gem was upside down, cushioned in my fist.

"It's just a big waste of money. Plus, you don't really have anyone to invite, anyway."

"What do you mean I don't have anyone to invite? We could do a small destination thing." I wasn't sure why I was now asking Mom for a wedding I was in charge of planning.

"And Rob's side of the church would be full of his friends and family, and your side will be Dad and me . . . and maybe Maxine and Garrett." She said it like it was a fact, something I already should have known.

"Rob wants a wedding, and his family will want a church wedding."

"Who are you going to invite? Lisa? You know, I still think she may be behind the identity theft. Or Nila? We can't trust them."

I realized my mom could go on like this, listing people we knew and then reminding me how estranged we were from them. Maybe she was right. Maybe planning a wedding would bring me nothing by heartache and humiliation. I wasn't convinced that night, but Mom reiterated her wish for us to elope about once a month for years.

With an unknown future in front of us, and two families fractured about the kind of ceremony we should have, we put off the wedding indefinitely. After a while it stopped mattering. Rob and the lovely ring were the two best things that I had. To want any more than that just seemed selfish.

TWENTY-FOUR

I WAITED MONTHS FOR the rejection letters. I was used to rejection letters by this point—for credit, for graduate school, for jobs—but it didn't make them any easier.

Several weeks after the proposal, on one of the first warm days of spring, I opened my mailbox to find a thin envelope from Iowa State. My heart sank. The thin envelopes always contained rejections. I tossed the letter like a Frisbee on the futon, wondering which version of the standard "We regret to inform you…" language this one would feature. I went into the kitchen to get something to drink, turning around to scowl at the ominous-looking letter as I filled a glass with tap water. *Just get it over with*, I chided myself.

I took a deep breath and opened the letter. This one was going to hurt.

"Congratulations!" it began. I had to read the word a few times before it translated into palpable joy I could feel in my chest. I'd been admitted to the program—with an assistantship—which meant I could *go* and not go broke.

Over the next month, I would collect more acceptance letters and not a single rejection.

* * *

My assistantship at Iowa State required me to work as an advisor for undergraduate students in the Family and Consumer Sciences Education and Studies program. I was good at this job, and soon word got out that I could help people who had had their identities stolen. My advisees began recommending to their friends to come see me if they, too, were dealing with credit card fraud or student loan fraud. In 2008, I won the American Association of Family and Consumer Sciences Outstanding Advisor award. I was coming into my own professionally, and I'd never felt anything so gratifying.

At the same time, I was also pitching my dissertation topics to potential advisors of my own. My idea was to conduct some sort of qualitative study on child identity theft victims to understand the impact of identity theft on this particular population. In other words, what—financially, psychologically, and emotionally—does identity theft do to a child? Like my master's work, part of the project was selfish, but part of it was about wanting to know myself better. I no longer felt guilty about it. Perhaps it was becoming a more experienced scholar, or maybe it was just growing up—but during those years I began to wrest control away from the faceless person who had stolen who I was. I was changing. I owned my own story now.

I secured an advisor and slowly began carving out a dissertation proposal between classes and work. However, my advisor retired, administrative changes occurred within the Family and Consumer Sciences Education program, and I found myself needing a new academic home three years into the program. I found it—just down the hall from my office, in the Human Development and Family Studies program.

The HDFS faculty were even more supportive of my dissertation topic. Slowly, I located individuals around the country who'd had their identities stolen as children but who didn't find out about it until they were adults. They were my subjects, not my friends, and I had to be very careful not to commiserate or compare notes. But they inspired me—the one who wasn't angry, the one who stalked her thief across the country, knocking on her front door to confront her. And just like I always had, I waited, scouring interview transcripts and research notes, for that one nugget of information that would lead me to my own redemption, or even a front-door confrontation.

My research earned me a place behind podiums at conferences and on panels at industry meetings. I presented at the American Council on Consumer Interests and the National Council on Family Relations conferences. I spoke at the Iowa Association of Family and Consumer Sciences and the Illinois Consumer Education Association conferences. I was invited to develop webinars for the Federal Reserve Bank of Minneapolis.

After I passed my comprehensive exams, I was ABD, all but dissertation, and ready to go on the market. I landed the first job I interviewed for.

In the summer of 2011, I packed my things in preparation for my move to Charleston, Illinois, where I would begin the following term as an assistant professor at Eastern Illinois University.

TWENTY-FIVE

By the summer I left Ames, I had been called upon a number of times as a field expert for articles and TV segments about identity theft. I'd like to say this was wholly thanks to my reputation; instead it happened as a result of me being a bit of a pest. As I began to claim more and more of my scholarly territory, I started noticing the errors and omissions that syndicate news stations and small-town newspapers were in the habit of making when they reported on identity theft. Unable to abide false or misleading information, and now feeling a sense of ownership about the topic, I would email the writer or reporter, tell them they got it wrong, and offer guidance on how to fix whatever *it* was. This led to many enthusiastic callbacks; experts on identity theft were still hard to find.

It felt great to be helping other people in need of these resources, like I had been all those years ago in West Lafayette, but one of these interviews was especially meaningful.

On a windy day in February, I pulled into the gated lot of WTHR, Channel 13 in downtown Indianapolis. I left the car running for the heat and grabbed the pouch of Cheerios

I had just bought from the twenty-four-hour Walgreens down
the street to calm my nerves. Looking up at the massive radio
antenna, I remembered the way the orange carpet would burn
my elbows after too long watching TV on the living room floor.
I remembered the "I hope you do" of approval Dad had made
when I said, "One day, I'm going to figure out who is doing
this to us and we won't have to live like this anymore." We had
been watching the evening news on WTHR, our nightly routine.
"And people will listen to me; I'll go on Channel 13 and talk
about it." My parents viewed Channel 13 as the beacon of truth
in the world.

Seventeen years later, I balanced my cell phone on my knee
as I dialed my mom's number on speaker. I got her voice mail.
"Hey, Mom. I'm here in the Channel 13 parking lot to talk
about identity theft, just like I said I would be when I was a
kid," I said, knowing she would hear the smile in my tone. "I
hope whoever stole our identities watches this."

After one more check of my hair and makeup, I stepped
outside to brave the familiar Indiana chill. The interview lasted
for about two hours. When it aired, the segment was about two
minutes long.

* * *

A couple of weeks later, over Spring break, I was with Mom at
her favorite diner in Albany. Flurries swirled around us as we
hugged in the parking lot. We stepped into Osborn's—a greasy
spoon Mom frequented with her girlfriends and old clients. It
was one of those breakfast-all-day places, the kind of Midwestern joints where gossip was passed around like the salt and
pepper. The humid air that met us at the door was heavy with

the smell of gravy and eggs. We made our way to a booth in the back, taking our places in front of paper place mats and thick, enamel coffee mugs.

"Oh, look, there's 'my farmer'!"

I swung my head around to see who Mom was pointing at, confused as to who she was referring to—after all, Dad should have been "her farmer." A group of men—obviously farmers—were congregated around a small table near the front of the diner.

"Who?"

"Let me introduce you!" she said, halfway out of the booth.

I followed behind her, weaving in and out of jacket-strewn seats. When we arrived at the table of men, I saw that they all wore the same familiar grin.

"Axton, meet my farmer friend! He's heard a lot about you." She moved out of the way so that I could shake the hand of this stranger, a man with tanned, leathery skin, even in the dead of winter.

"Nice to meet you, young lady."

"He has been a lot of help with the commodities class I'm teaching in Marion," Mom explained. She had just picked up the adjunct position that term, leveraging her experience as a stockbroker who knew a little about farm futures and options.

"Ah," I said, not knowing what else to say. I felt the eyes of the other men burning through me. A few of them were snickering. Some old men didn't know how to act around anyone younger than thirty, I supposed.

"Did you watch Channel 13 a couple of weeks ago like I told you to? Axton did an interview!"

I smiled and nodded.

"I only watch Channel 8," this new friend told me. At first I thought it was a joke, but when I smiled at him, he didn't reflect my amusement.

"Okay, we'll let you boys get back to your meal. Nice seeing you!" Mom grabbed my arm and led me back to our table. Over lunch, she filled me in on all the latest local gossip.

I was staying with Mom and Dad in Redkey over break. I hadn't been home in a while—my dissertation and a full-time teaching load had been stealing all my time—but I knew from many phone calls that it had been a transitional year for them both. The heart-pounding crises of my youth—the cops at the door, the foreclosure notices—had, from what I heard, pretty much stopped when I left for school. But the phone calls, the delinquent account slips and court summonses, those still arrived in Mom's PO Box daily. On top of that, Mom had been let go from her beloved job at Q95 after a management shake-up. At first she had been reassigned to the station's front desk, dealing mostly with the strange collection of people who win call-in contests for concert tickets. But eventually she was laid off from even that indecorous role. It was a far fall from power, but I had been impressed with how she seemed to take it in stride. After stints working for one of the station's advertisers and then a cable company, she settled in for a while as a cashier at a farm supply store.

My mother had been professionally unfulfilled for my entire life. As I moved through my graduate work, I began to understand what it meant to do what you love, to feel called to your profession. It made me sad that Mom never seemed to have felt that. I tried to be extra available to talk during this time, just in case I could help her somehow.

"I could do more if I had a master's degree. I should have gotten the degree," she told me one night at the table. She looked older under the glow of the dining room chandelier. The white of her hair showed through fading dye like Christmas tree tinsel.

"Listen, Mom. I'm almost thirty. You can't use me as an excuse anymore. You can't use Dad as an excuse anymore. It's time to just do it. Take out the loans. Go full-time for two years. And then get a job you actually like." I figured if anyone could take tough love, it would be Mom. She had been dishing it out for decades.

Mom sighed and pursed her lips to one side. I knew she had been envious of my academic success; she had always been proud of her own undergraduate education, how the professors in her male-dominated field had told her she didn't belong there, how she had proved them all wrong.

"But your dad—"

"Who cares what Dad thinks? Go do what you want."

Our relationship was unconventional—this kind of conversation was as close as we came to a heart-to-heart—but I was proud of how honest we could be with each other.

And I was doubly proud when Mom enrolled once again at Ball State, to pursue her master's in adult and higher education. Dad was even on board. He said that when school started, her years-long bad mood began to lift. If she was happy, he was happy.

Dad was also going through changes at his job. The store where he had been produce manager for nearly two decades closed and he was sent to work at another location as an assistant produce manager. If I knew one thing about my dad, it was that he would be a good assistant *nothing*. Dad was the boss, through and through. Eventually he was reassigned to yet another store, but this time back in his usual role.

He was still feeling a lot of worry, though, he said, mostly about my mother's health. She had been feeling off for many months: her muscles hurt and her legs would jerk as if she was undergoing a reflex test. Disconcertingly, this would happen a lot while she drove. Then came the night sweats, which the doctors had assured her was simply menopause. When she started experiencing frequent fevers, the doctors rescinded their earlier conclusion, hypothesizing that she might have a heart condition. Sometimes she told me it felt as if she'd been poisoned. I couldn't do much from four hours away in Charleston but I called home often, mostly to let Mom know I was thinking of her.

TWENTY-SIX

IN CHARLESTON, ILLINOIS, the hardwood forests of the East fold into the grassy prairies and quilted farmland that stretch all the way to the Rocky Mountains. It is a small city, smaller than Ames, but larger than Portland and Havana combined. The most notable residents of Charleston are the some seven thousand undergrads of Eastern Illinois University and the ghost of Abraham Lincoln. His presence is palpable here, at his log cabin, his parents' homestead, the courthouse where he famously debated Stephen Douglas, where he worked through his own ambivalence—and talking points—about racial equality.

When I arrived in Charleston, it was with a profound excitement for my first "real" job and the anxiety that always trailed not far behind. Sure, I had made it through my coursework and checked off my exams, but I still had a dissertation to write. If I didn't finish my PhD within a year of my appointment at EIU, I would be promptly dismissed. Luckily, there wasn't too much about the town that would distract me from my work. It was a lot like the other Midwestern towns I had left behind— some rusty downtown charm and the inevitable strip of fast-food restaurants out on the highway. Even Rob was now three hours away, near the Quad Cities, taking on *his* first big job, too. We knew marriage was in our future, but remained ever practical: we'd get our careers on solid footing first and figure out the rest later. By then, long-distance was second nature to us.

Although I had now been, in some capacity, a fixture of academia for a decade, the job at EIU was my first introduction to a teaching-intensive university, where the typical teaching load is 4-4, or four classes a semester. It was a sharp adjustment. Research, while a requirement, was deemphasized in the name of teaching and service. There were times when I felt many of my coworkers were judging me for pursuing research. I was told that it was a distraction from the "real work" I was supposed to be doing in the classroom and on various student and department-centered committees. I learned quickly to keep my research agenda to myself and began looking outside EIU for collaboration opportunities. During the day I was a devoted teacher and faculty member; at night I was a student again, working feverishly to hone my scholarship. Looking back, I guess I should have felt torn into many pieces, but I was used to that feeling.

In summer 2012, after my first year at EIU, I was invited to be part of a national research team to use phenomenology to study elder financial exploitation within families. The similarities between this work and my dissertation were strong, and it seemed like I could be an asset to the team. I accepted the invitation and began working with the group, presenting and publishing with them, keeping quiet about it around campus.

It was a convenient coincidence that members of the team were slated to present at the same national conference in Indianapolis where I was to receive an award for my child identity theft research and outreach activities. This award would be particularly poignant because Mom and Dad would be in the audience. I knew Mom wasn't feeling well and that the two-hour car ride from Redkey would be a challenge. But when I met them in the hotel lobby, she seemed a little worse for wear but so happy to be there. That evening we posed for pictures, my parents flanking me as I proudly held up my award, my mother positively beaming.

Mom and Dad and me at the AAFCS ceremony.

* * *

The date on my transcript says August 4, 2012. That's the day I became Dr. Axton Betz. It should have been one of the best days of my life. Instead, I will always remember it as trading one torturous slog—completing the dissertation—with another, even more hellacious marathon.

Mom had called on the first day of August. It was steamy in Illinois, a day that made winter seem like a distant and impossible memory. She said she had a heat rash, she thought, but what really worried her was the grapefruit-sized lump in the fleshy part of her upper arm.

"I think it might be cancer," she said.

I turned those words over in my mind for a few seconds. Mom couldn't have cancer. She was invincible. A force. I had never entertained the idea that my mother might be mortal. But then another thought barged in—Mom was fifty-six. Grandma was fifty-six when she died of breast cancer. Was that some cursed year in our family? Was Mom's number up?

She told me she had an appointment with a new doctor in a few days and was confident he would get to the bottom of it. When we hung up, I tried to channel her confidence.

What happened next is hazy, communicated to me through a frenzy of panicked calls. Day and night blurred together; I lived with the phone in my hand.

Dad said the day after Mom and I had spoken, she began complaining of severe pain and trouble breathing. She needed to go to the emergency room, the one in Indy where there were specialists. They got in the car but Mom couldn't make it—she felt like she was dying. So they stopped in Muncie, where she was admitted to Ball Memorial Hospital. The next forty-eight hours were a flurry of blood tests and examinations, as the staff tried to solve the puzzle of weird symptoms Mom had been experiencing for months. The waiting and uncertainty swallowed large chunks of time. I had so much work to do, but for the life of me I couldn't figure out how to sit down at my desk and do it.

At last, Dad called with definitive news.

"They think she has a blood infection. Not cancer!"

My relief was audible.

"She'll probably be here for about a week, so I'm going home to get her some clothes."

If Dad felt buoyant enough to leave Mom alone in the hospital for an hour or two, I reasoned that I, too, could finally relax. Just a blood infection; she was going to be fine. I could get to work on the upcoming semester's syllabi. But fifteen minutes later, the phone rang again. It was Mom.

"Well, I have an official diagnosis," she said weakly.

"I know—Dad told me! You have a blood infection and you'll be just fine in a week or so!"

There were a few seconds of silence then, as if the universe needed a moment to rearrange everything just so. My relief turned to despair; my reality shifted.

"I have leukemia."

My legs shook like I had just narrowly avoided a car accident. I tightened my grip on the phone.

"They can't handle it here. I'm going by ambulance to IU in Indy."

Nothing was making sense. "No, Mom. Dad said you have a blood infection. You'll be fine in a week." Tears slid down my cheeks. I walked to the back patio door and opened it, but the afternoon air hung still and stifling.

"This isn't a death sentence, Axton. People recover from leukemia."

There were more phone calls—one from Dad, one to Rob—I don't remember what we said and I probably wouldn't want to if I could.

Burkitt's acute lymphoblastic leukemia is very rare in the United States—only a couple thousand people are diagnosed each year. It is an extremely aggressive lymphoma, but treatable if diagnosed early. Mom was right: people do survive. But after a lifetime of bad luck and misfortune, I didn't know if the optimistic statistics I found online could possibly apply to us.

I turned the ringer on my phone off. I couldn't talk or take any more. My anxiety ratcheted up and up, like it did that day in the chapel, that afternoon in animal science class I wanted to shed my skin, get out of my own body. I sat on my porch, swatting gnats, until the sun went down, searching for the stars between the trees. Something moved in me and I spoke to them out loud.

"If you can hear me, wherever you are." I knew without thinking that I was speaking to my grandparents, Mom's parents. "I need you to send in reinforcements because it's just me and Dad and we cannot do this on our own."

I remembered the afternoon Mom and I had spent in Indian Lake, how she drove through the neighborhood looking for her parents, like she might find them there walking down the street, her mother's pearls shining and my grandfather clad in his dress slacks. I never knew if she felt like she had found them that day, or communed with them in any way. But now I hoped she had. That the lines of communication were open. That they could save her like she had so desperately wanted to save them.

I didn't care what the neighbors thought; I inflated my air mattress and slung it out onto the porch. Being outside was the only way I felt like I could breathe. It was the first night of the shallow and halting sleep I would endure for months. Around sunrise I was roused by the haunting cries of mourning doves, my hand still clutching a silent phone.

TWENTY-SEVEN

FOR THE NEXT SIX MONTHS of my life, many of the moments that mattered—or the ones I remember anyway—happened on my cell phone. Like the stool-bound phone of my youth, my cell often seemed my only source of gravity. Rob and I visited each other as much as possible, and I was teaching a full load of classes, but the only thing that gave me weight were the updates I was getting from Dad. My cell phone became an extension of my body, so much so that I changed the technology clause in my syllabi from *never ever* to *we all have things we need to take care of.* I often took phone calls from Dad in the middle of a lecture, just in case.

* * *

"Thirty days at IU, two weeks at home," he had said, like he was memorizing his new schedule. "She'll get inpatient chemo at IU, and then outpatient chemo in Muncie while she's back. And we'll do that for six months."

It was just a few days after I slept on my porch. I liked this plan, the rigidity of it; in the midst of this upheaval, a routine was welcome.

"The doctors say she has an eighty percent chance of survival," Dad said with as much good cheer as he could muster. I knew he was beyond tired; his last few days had been a series of laps around central Indiana: Mom, work at the store, work on the farm, a few hours of rest, repeat. But 80 percent sounded like a good number. Maybe Mom was right. Maybe people do recover from leukemia. Maybe she would be one of those people.

I told him to think positive thoughts, and to get some sleep.

* * *

"A customer gave me this book—it's about healing cancer the natural way, without all the chemicals and radiation," he said with a note of excitement. I was on my couch grading in Illinois and happy my father couldn't detect my eye-rolling. He had always been a clean eater: very little meat and few processed foods.

"I'm trying to convince her to consider an all-natural diet. She can't really eat right now anyway; there's too much pain in her jaw. I bought a Ninja juicer and it's waiting for her at home—"

"Dad, do you really think Mom is going to go for that?" My mother was a notoriously bad eater: When Dad and I would eat vegetables, Mom would wrinkle her nose and have meat instead. She would claim her eating habits were part of her Midwestern identity and being a "corn-fed woman."

"If she wants to live, she will!"

I let him tell me more about alternative healing, silently wondering when Mom would call, outraged and disgusted by my father's proposed diet.

* * *

"Can you see what's on your Mom's Facebook page?"

"No, everything is set to private." I didn't tell him I could "friend" my mother on Facebook if I wanted to, because I didn't want to. I wasn't hiding anything, just trying to avoid her prying eyes or embarrassing comments. Our digital lives were better left separate, I thought.

"She's always on that goddamn computer. What could she possibly need to be on there so much for? When I come in from the barn, or from work, she snaps her computer shut as fast as she can. I ask her what she's doing and she says homework!"

"To be fair, she is taking that online course. She probably has a lot of discussion forums to post to. I wouldn't worry about it."

I chalked up Dad's concern to naivete about graduate school in the twenty-first century and his own lack of experience with using the internet. From what I could tell, Mom seemed to have dived headfirst into graduate school in spite of battling leukemia.

There was silence while he considered this. I stared at the eggshell walls of my living room.

"You really think so?"

"Yeah, definitely."

"She can put the laundry in, but she can't bend down to get it and put it in the dryer," Dad said, seemingly cured of his suspicion. "We have this system where she puts it in in the morning, and I come home and finish the job in the afternoon. Teamwork."

I knew he was trying to convince me they were fine, but every minute I spent in Charleston felt like a small betrayal. I wanted to be near my mother.

* * *

"Your mom shaved her head." Mom had been through a partial round of inpatient chemo. Dad had been warning me about her appearance.

"I know. She said it was easier than waiting for her hair to fall out."

"She got the nurses to put this sign up on the door; you'll see it. It says *Restricted Visitors*. Only me, you, Rob, Michelle, and your uncle Larry are allowed in."

I paused and looked up from the kitchen table, where I had been sitting, textbooks and papers strewn about. "Um, are you guys having a problem with visitors?" Knowing how much my mom loved attention, I was surprised to hear she wasn't entertaining guests at her bedside.

"She said they'll all be coming in to sightsee, as she puts it. To see how bad she looks."

I frowned at this news.

"She said Maxine is depressing anyway. That is her word: 'depressing.' You know I don't know those people. It's whatever she wants."

* * *

I tried not to stare the first time I walked into her room. Mom was a ghostly white, her face seemingly swollen, maybe from all the saline they were pushing through her. But she was wearing a full face of makeup. Around her, machines buzzed and hissed, connected to her via a web of wires and tubes that ran beneath a thin, white blanket tucked under her sides like a harness. I thought of what Dad said about people "sightseeing" and moved my eyes quickly from her face to the wide window that over-looked downtown Indianapolis as my anxiety started to ratchet up. *This is real*, I thought to myself.

"Hey, I brought you some things," I said, trying to sound cheerful as I moved toward her. I felt Mom's eyes on me as I carefully set up framed photos of my cats, who she jokingly called her grandcats, next to the one taken just six weeks before, of us in Indianapolis at the award ceremony. When the cancer was colonizing inside of Mom but we didn't know it yet. I turned around to see her smiling at the photos as best she could. The disease had practically paralyzed the nerves in her jaw, mouth, and cheeks.

TWENTY-EIGHT

HERE'S WHAT WAS SUPPOSED to happen: Mom would endure six months of her chemo regimen; it would be grueling but it would be effective. Afterward, she would enter remission, remaining cancer-free for about five years until the doctors considered her cured. Then we would all go back to our regularly scheduled life.

Here's what actually happened: Mom's Burkitt's quickly revealed itself to be a chemo-resistant strain of the disease. The doctors told us this was very rare and that, while she needed to continue treatment, she would also need a bone marrow transplant. The bone marrow match would have to be nearly perfect in order for her body to accept it, and because Mom only had half siblings, there was no one in the family who could provide that match. We launched into PR mode for Mom; Dad told nearly everyone who walked into the store about Mom's illness and I covered my Facebook wall in "Be The Match" literature.

Even if a match would have showed up in the database, Mom's eligibility kept getting pushed back when, invariably, another infection would commandeer her body. These infections came one right after the other, like violent ocean waves, and were terrifying in that they could easily spawn full-blown pneumonia, an illness that could be fatal in Mom's fragile state. Dad and I obsessively applied hand sanitizer up to our elbows, and carried it with us everywhere. The consoles of my car were sanitizer-bottle cemeteries, and I double-pumped the extra-large bottle of Sea Island Cotton sanitizer at my desk at least twice an hour. I made it very clear to my students that if they were the least bit sick, they needed to stay home.

The physical—and psychological—seesaw we were riding took an immediate toll on Dad. Fatigue enveloped him like a thick mist and even when he was in the room he seemed far away and fuzzy. On top of his frenzied schedule—a full-time job, a herd of animals, a suffering wife, and many miles of interstate between him and his next obligation—he was now shouldering their financial obligations. Medical bills began piling up, for what the insurance companies wouldn't cover, and though Mom insisted on helping out by still making sure everything got paid on time, I could tell the anxiety of it all was having its way with my father. He lost weight. The skin below his eyes grew thin and dark. I forgot what his smile looked like.

As for me, I felt lucky that I had a job that required my full engagement. It kept me occupied during the hours I couldn't be at the hospital or on the phone with my dad. Speaking at conferences, in front of a crowd, was the one time I could shut everything else out and simply focus on the moment, on my talk and the questions that followed. For fifteen brief and wonderful minutes, I could be normal. And then the next presenter would get up to speak and reality would inevitably reclaim me.

One particularly poignant—and unexpected—talk I gave that

winter was at my alma mater Jay County High School. I was Facebook friends with a few current and retired teachers there, and when they saw I was presenting on financial safety and identity theft around the country, they reached out and asked if I might speak to upperclassmen about similar topics. Although walking back into that school felt like a panic attack waiting to happen, I agreed to the talk, solely for the excuse to visit Mom on a legitimate work trip.

Nothing looked the same except the outside of the brick building. The blue lockers were now red, the hallways were freshly painted, and even the smell I remembered had been replaced by the heavy scents of lacquer and printer paper. The faculty directory listed very few familiar names. Surprisingly, I did not endure crippling anxiety upon entering the building; I guess I had bigger things to worry about now. I couldn't help but pause to reflect on how much had changed, how much *I* had changed since I left more than a decade ago.

I made back-to-back presentations, in which I instructed the students to be wary of what they put on social media for all to see, to not be lured into thinking that identity theft would never happen to them. "I never thought it would happen to me, either," I said. The audience of young eyes looked back at me with incredulity; I hoped some of what I was saying was getting through to them.

Afterward, on the way to the hospital, I made a detour to the cemetery where Mom's parents were buried. Since that night on the porch I had thought about them often, as if I were waiting for some kind of dramatic intervention from above. So far, I had been disappointed.

The black marble headstone they shared was right where I remembered it—adjacent to the main road that bisects Green

Park Cemetery. At first I spoke softly, greeting them as if they were sitting in front of me. But soon I was hissing in frustration, my black flats digging deeper into the soggy ground.

"Goddammit, Dad can't go on like this!" I yelled. "And I can't, either!"

A subtle movement on the horizon caught my attention. An elderly woman walking a small white dog was staring at me with concern.

With as much dignity as I could muster, I buttoned my tan trench coach and slid back into the driver's seat. Forty minutes later I was at the hospital in Muncie.

* * *

It was the night before New Year's Eve when I shot straight up in bed, immediately wondering what it was that woke me. And then I felt it: the sudden punch of pain in my stomach.

My first thought was Mom. I had planned to spend my birthday with her in Indiana in just a few days, but I couldn't go there with the stomach flu. Slowly, I pushed myself out of bed and lurched downstairs. I stood on my patio wrapped in an afghan—maybe it was my childhood on the farm but fresh air always seemed like the first course of treatment. Watching my breath unfurl in front of me, I fretted: *What if this is my last chance to spend my birthday with both my parents?* I willed the bad thoughts—and nausea—to pass.

A few days and many ginger ales later, I felt well enough to work on my annual review. The sharp and persistent pain in my stomach had moved to the hollow of my ribs, so intense that I would have suspected my appendix if I still had one. I slammed my fingers against the keyboard, doing my best to ignore the pain, until I couldn't anymore. Whatever was in my stomach was making it very clear that it did not intend to stay there.

I pushed my computer aside and stood up, meaning to make my way to the bathroom. But I had waited too long. I retched violently. I threw up nothing but stomach acid and as a gush of blood ran down my legs.

Alone and panicked, it was pure adrenaline that carried me upstairs and into a hot bath. But moments later I was throwing up again, and still bleeding. I didn't dare call Dad, he had enough to worry about, and I knew Rob would tell me to go to the ER. Instead, I fell asleep in my bed holding a pillow against my tender abdomen. In the morning, I relented and drove myself to the doctor.

The doctors found a benign tumor, and could offer no explanation as to why it had appeared, other than perhaps it was hereditary. To me, the growth seemed like an obvious manifestation of the fear and anxiety I had been carrying around for so many years.

I was bedbound for a week. I spent my thirty-first birthday alone.

TWENTY-NINE

THE DRIVE TO WASHINGTON, DC, had been precarious. Relentless snow and freezing rain had transformed the interstate into an icy washboard. My white-knuckled journey had been punctuated by calls from Mom, who was home again and sounding disoriented—and from Dad, who sounded desperately worried about Mom. In the Allegheny Mountains I had to pull over and wait for a snowplow to clear the way. Every mile was a struggle; each minute that passed I suppressed dread for my own safety and for Mom's worsening prognosis. When I finally made it to DC, the sight of the glowing monuments against the February night sky felt downright triumphant.

Even if my personal life had not been a maze of grief and confusion, the trek to DC would have been nerve-wracking—because of the weather, but *especially* because of why I was going. The Identity Theft Assistance Center's national forum on child identity theft was the most prestigious speaking engagement I had ever booked. The offices of the center were sandwiched between the White House and the Capitol, and the conference had drawn personnel from the FBI, the DOJ, and other major players in identity theft policy and advocacy. This would be far from the academic crowd I was used to. I had been invited to share a little of my personal story as well as my dissertation research.

One of many presentations on identity theft and its insidious consequences.

That night in the hotel I was restless. My nerves were still buzzing from the road, and sleep was elusive. Light from the street infiltrated the cracks in the curtains and I felt nostalgic for the days when I used to sleep soundly and easily. Now, when I did sleep, I often woke up crying. Less sleep did mean more time to work, and the previous semester had been one of the most productive of my career. It turned out that avoiding the enormity of Mom's mortality took hours of my undivided attention.

The next day, on just three hours of sleep, I made my way to ITAC. The conference room was intimidating. There were microphones on every table, making the space feel more like a Senate hearing than a research forum. Cameras stood in the back of the room and conference-call speakers dotted the presenters' table. My talk would be heard around the country. When it was my turn, I straightened my black suit jacket, pushed down my anxiety, and enjoyed my fifteen minutes of normalcy.

After my talk, all I could think about was calling Dad. Our conversations the day before had been upsetting. At this point, Mom was receiving daily radiation treatments, and not doing well at all. He thought that she was losing her will to keep going. That morning, while I gave my talk, she had received her thirteenth round of radiation out of a prescribed eighteen. I found a quiet space in the hallway outside the conference room and started dialing Dad's number.

"Hello? Axton?" said an unfamiliar voice behind me. I turned around to see a man with broad shoulders, brown hair, and a homecoming-king smile.

"My name is Joe Mason—I wrote about you in my book." He said this as if it were a completely normal way to introduce yourself to someone. I put my phone back in my bag and shook the man's hand with, I'm sure, a bewildered look on my face.

"You've got to be kidding me," I said, wondering what kind of scam this was. "I have to see this."

"Follow me back to my table and I'll show you."

I followed him back to a stack of books, where he picked one up, holding it out for me.

"It's called *Bankrupt at Birth* and there are two pages in here dedicated to your story." On the front cover, a young girl with long brunette hair sat, arms crossed, behind a smashed piggy bank. I was still getting my conversational bearings, but I wanted to tell Mr. Mason that the image did little to convey the devastating nature of identity theft.

"Show me, please," I said instead, growing excited about taking the book to Mom. Surely, this would lift her spirits. I held the book open while Joe flipped to the right place. There, spread across pages twenty-nine and thirty, was my story. Culled from the various media reports I had taken part in, the account was almost completely accurate. Twenty years of my life in two pages. It was surreal. I had to call Dad. I thanked Joe and we said we'd be in touch.

"It didn't go well this morning," Dad said when I got him on the phone. "She's in a lot of pain."

"Dad," I said, still buoyed from seeing my name in print. "Just tell Mom our case has been written about in a book. I'm bringing a copy home to show her."

When the forum was over, I walked around DC, to the places I'd been on the field trip with Heritage Hall, before identity theft had bruised everything, before Mom was sick. I walked past Ford's Theatre and wished Mom, a self-proclaimed history buff, was with me. A bitter wind whipped off the Potomac and tore down the National Mall as I passed the Capitol Building and made my way to the Washington Monument. I felt my face burn red and I burrowed my chin deeper into the collar of my trench coat. I knew I couldn't stay out long, but being written about in a book felt like a reason to celebrate. Some good in a season of nothing but bad news.

When I got back to my room, I checked the weather. I wasn't eager to be in the car again, battling icy interstates, but I felt a deep compulsion to get home to Mom. Another snowstorm was threatening the mid-Atlantic, so I decided to leave before dawn and take the southern route through Tennessee and Virginia. It would add about five hours to my trip, but would ensure I didn't get stuck in some forgotten mountain town.

The next day, after more than five hundred miles, one speeding ticket, and hours of squinting at the double yellow line to keep it still, I stopped in southern Kentucky for the night. In the morning, while I was navigating a frenzied Cincinnati rush hour, Dad called.

"I thought you'd be farther along in your trip than you are," he said, sounding annoyed.

"How did radiation go?" I said, deflecting, trying to change lanes and maintain my speed.

"Not good. Your mom didn't even want to go. She's asleep in bed now so I'm going to work for a couple of hours. You need to get home."

When my dad said this to me—"You need to get home"— I felt like I had been fighting for days, for months. Fighting weather, fighting traffic, fighting the unrelenting panic buried deep in my chest. I was wrung out and scared, and yet there was nothing I could do about any of it. The weather and traffic were well out of my control. The panic—how else was I supposed to feel with my mom dying slowly in her bed? Of course I needed to get home. Did my dad think I didn't know this? "I'll be there as soon as I can," I said, and floored it.

When I pulled in the driveway, I called Mom.

"I'm here. Can you let me in?" I never had my damn house key; I hadn't seen it since the move to Illinois.

"I don't think I can do that," she whimpered. I ran around back to find the spare in one of the farm's outbuildings. I fumbled with it in the front door, my hands trembling from hours on the road. I walked briskly to the spare room where Mom was staying. When I saw her, rolled half over in bed, arms outstretched toward her walker, alarm flooded my body. She looked terrible.

"Do you need help, Mom?" I said, rushing over to her.

"No. Yeah. No. Yeah, just grab my leg." She was wincing

in pain. The navy-checked sheets at her feet were bound up in knots. Pill bottles littered the end table.

"You want me to put it on the floor? Just balance on me," I said, and leaned over so she could put her hands on my shoulders.

"No," she said firmly. "Put me back in bed."

"Mom, are you giving up?" I asked calmly, though I wanted to yell. I wanted to shake her and tell her how much I had dealt with to get to her side. I wanted to let her know that she—and I—had come too far to give up now.

"No. Just call your dad," she said, with her eyes open wide and wearing a painful grimace. She began to knead her chest with both hands.

"What's the matter? Is it anxiety? Did you push yourself too hard trying to get up?"

"This happens," she managed. I had no idea what "this" was.

I went into the den and pulled Joe Mason's book out of my suitcase. Back in her bedroom, Mom was still clutching at her chest. I stood next to her. "This is called *Bankrupt at Birth*, Mom, and I'm in here." I held up the book like a kindergarten teacher for her to see. I opened to page twenty-nine and started reading.

"'Axton Betz never suspected she had a problem until the day she rented her first off-campus apartment,'" I began.

My mother looked at me with pained but proud eyes and whispered, "That's so great, honey." She kept her gaze directed at me as I went on.

"Do you feel better?" I asked when I had finished. She shook her head. "Do you want me to call Dad? We can take you to the hospital?" I offered, poised to run and get my phone.

"I need to go by ambulance." The words landed like an

anchor. Why had she lain there listening to me read if she knew she needed to go to the hospital this urgently?

I called Dad. I called the Cancer Center at Ball Memorial. I called Dad again. I paced back and forth. I called an ambulance. I hauled the rugs and my suitcases away from the front door so the paramedics would have a clear path. In a few minutes I would wave them in like a restaurant hostess and say "first door on the left."

But now, in the meantime, I walked back to Mom's room, and sat beside her for what would be our last moments together at home. Soon, the convoy of sirens filled the house like an oncoming storm.

THIRTY

FROM HER HOSPITAL BED, Mom sent me home. She had been there overnight and when Dad and I arrived first thing in the morning, she told us the doctors were optimistic she'd be going home in two to three days. She told me to go back to Illinois and return the rental car I'd been driving and she wanted Dad to go to work. I felt a little uneasy as I drove out of Muncie that day, but Mom insisted she would be fine.

I had been in Charleston long enough to return the rental car when Dad called. I answered the phone poised above my half-unpacked suitcase. He sputtered like an engine that couldn't catch. I could tell that whatever it was, it was very bad.

"They...said there's nothing else they can do for your mom. You need to come back. You have to come back home."

It took Rob three and a half hours to drive from East Moline to Charleston. The only thing I asked was that he bring a suit appropriate for both a wedding and a funeral. Nearly paralyzed with grief, I delayed our trip back to Indiana until the next morning. I managed to make phone calls to my cousin Michelle in Chicago and Uncle Larry in Ohio. I repacked the clothes I had been unpacking when Dad had called. I placed my doctoral gown on top of my suitcase. It was the most formal outfit I had; it would have to do.

* * *

The fifth floor of Ball Memorial smelled like sanitizer and cafeteria food. When Rob and I walked into Mom's room, Dad wasn't there. He had gone home to feed the animals. My mother was sprawled out on the hospital bed, beneath the strange glow of fluorescent lights. Channel 13 was on TV. I wondered if it was possible that her appearance had withered even more in just twenty-four hours. Tangles of tubes and wires emerged from underneath the sheets. Her eyes shifted and sparked slightly when we entered, and she weakly said hi.

I suddenly felt awkward, like I was trying to talk to a stranger at a party. "So, Dad told me . . . " I trailed off. Mom nodded her head. "Is there anything you want me to know? To do?" I set my purse down on the dialysis chair and approached her side. Rob stood silently at the foot of the bed.

"That I love you," she said quietly. "And you have to take care of your dad."

"Okay, I will." I studied the skin on her face. It was as if someone had switched off the light that had been behind it all these years.

"You'll be okay, but your dad won't be. Just take care of your dad."

I was bewildered, but I tried to reassure her. "Mom, Dad's a big boy; he can take care of himself. What is it I'm supposed to take care of—did you not pay a bill or something?" Bills, payments, deadlines—this was the language that my family had communicated in for my entire life. It would not have struck me as odd if my mom were talking to me about these subjects on her deathbed.

Mom's eyes rolled back in a flash of anger. She insisted, "Just...take...care...of your dad."

I looked at Rob, wordlessly communicating my confusion. He shrugged.

"Listen," I said, "Rob and I are going to get married, right here, Monday morning."

She opened her eyes, suddenly lucid again, and with concern said, "You guys need to have the wedding you want. Don't rush this."

"You don't get a say in this, Mom. Seven years doesn't seem like a rush. All I need you to do is still be here on Monday morning, okay?"

Rob and I settled into the room. Dad came back from the farm. His face was red and wrecked. Hospice nurses filed in and out of the room, making Mom comfortable with morphine and Dilaudid. They asked us if we were eating and drinking; they gave us a pamphlet on what to ask a loved one before they die.

"What do you want in your obituary, Mom?" I asked her, pausing on a page in the pamphlet. Intellectually, I understood how upsetting this conversation should be. But my emotions couldn't seem to keep pace with reality. And when I asked her how she wanted her life to be summarized in three or four paragraphs, I said it like I wanted her opinion on what we should have for dinner.

"I already told your dad. I don't want one." She shifted her head away from me, as if to end the conversation. This didn't surprise me. Dad had mentioned that she also asked there be no visitation, no funeral, and that we simply donate her body to science.

"Okay, we'll go with whatever you told him then," I said. If my mother wanted to disappear into the ether, who was I to object? Still, there were keepsakes I wanted.

"Mom, I want to borrow your wedding ring. To use it in the ceremony Monday." I hadn't seen my mother wear her wedding band in some time, and I assumed it was because the medicine had been making her fingers swell. "Can you tell me where it is?"

"The prongs are loose," she explained, her eyebrows furrowed with concentration, "but you can find it in the first drawer in my jewelry armoire." I could visualize just the spot in her dresser she was talking about; I had taken rings from there before.

Dad sent us home a few hours later, to rest and see to some chores on the farm. Rob and I collapsed into bed together, our nerves shattered from a long drive and longer afternoon. The night was frigid and still, and when the sun came up the next morning, Saturday, frost clung to every blade of brown grass. After I checked on the animals, we returned dutifully to the hospital. We spent the day sitting at my mother's bedside, watching Channel 13, and making sure she was comfortable. I was in touch with my dad's friend, a minister, charting out the details for Monday's ceremony. When my cousin Michelle arrived from Chicago, she was a welcome reinforcement. We took turns in shifts to get food, at the insistence of the hospice workers, despite our lack of appetite.

I didn't take well to people telling me to eat. Not eating was generally how I handled hard times. In the hospital cafeteria, I picked up a fruit cup that I had no interest in eating while Rob chose a hot meal.

After one bite, I told Rob, "I can't eat this."

"You have to," Rob said.

"My mother is lying upstairs dying and yet everyone is so concerned that I choke down this fucking fruit cup?"

"You need it. For your strength," Rob replied with the kind of evenness I loved him for.

The next morning, we prepared ourselves for a similar regimen. Later in the afternoon, however, one of Mom's nurses asked to speak with me in the hallway. She was aware that Rob and I were planning a wedding for the following day but wasn't sure we should wait.

"We don't think your mom is going to be conscious tomorrow," she said. I felt adrenaline rush up my spine. I clutched at my purse, mindful of the bottle of anxiety medication I had been leaning on, hard, during the last few days. "We have a chaplain on staff and he is available tonight. I would strongly urge you to consider getting married tonight."

I nodded, heard myself say something, and then walked into Mom's room. "Mom, the nurses think we should push up the wedding. They don't think you will be conscious tomorrow. What do you think? You know your body. Should we get married tomorrow or do it tonight?"

"Tonight," she said, without hesitation.

"Okay, we'll do it tonight."

We had a handful of hours, but Rob and I raced back to the farm. On the way I called Dad, who was in the barn feeding the animals, and told him the new plan.

"Who in the hell's idea is this?" he shouted. I hadn't heard my dad this on edge since the day he opened the foreclosure notice, which by now was fourteen years ago. Everything was shifting around him and I knew his already-low capacity for change was at a breaking point.

"It's Mom's idea, Dad."

"Oh. I'll start getting ready then."

Once home, we scrambled to get everything together. I followed Dad into the bedroom. When I opened the first drawer under the jewelry compartment, the ring was not there. "Dad, do you know where Mom's wedding ring is?"

"I don't know, Axton. I haven't seen it since before she got sick," he said, distracted, as he picked out a shirt.

"Well, she said it would be right here"—I pointed to the open drawer—"and it's not. I need it."

"Your mother is on heavy morphine," he said, growing impatient with me, "so maybe she thought it would be right there. But it's not right there. Just pick any ring out of there and we'll find it later."

I didn't want to see my father any more harried, but disappointment rang through me like church bells. With my fingertips, I sorted through the piles of costume jewelry she had accumulated from the TV over the years, looking for something that would make sense as a wedding ring. Beneath a showy broach I found a ring made of two bands, both in a cheap, brassy-looking gold. One band had a semi-circle of what had to be fake diamonds, and the other—made to lock into and on top of the first—was a large, fake diamond. The pair looked like an engagement and wedding band set, and though they were enormous on my finger, I pocketed them for the ceremony. I told myself that I would find the real thing later, and that right now all that mattered was Mom seeing us get married.

At the hospital later that night, the nurses let me use an empty hospital room as my dressing room. I put on my graduation gown: it was red with black stripes on the arms; a velvety, blue hood hung around my neck and reached down my back. My octagonal cap was made of felt, and looked vaguely like a court jester's. Michelle helped me get dressed. I felt like I was going to throw up. I popped a fourth anxiety pill, even though I wasn't supposed to take more than three per day.

When I entered my mother's room for the ceremony, it had been transformed. The nurses had pooled their own money to buy Valentine's Day decorations during the hour we had gone home to get our clothes. Glittery bows and tinsel hung from the walls. Vinyl heart decals, stuck to the window, stood out against the early evening dark. Cupcakes and sparkling juice had been set on a table, awaiting a reception. And scattered rose petals atop a white bedsheet became my impromptu aisle.

We all just barely held it together. The hospital chaplain was familiar and kind. Rob and I stumbled nervously through our vows. Dad took photos, hiding his welling eyes behind the camera. Michelle may have been the only matron of honor to ever wear sweatpants. The nurses eavesdropped from the hallway.

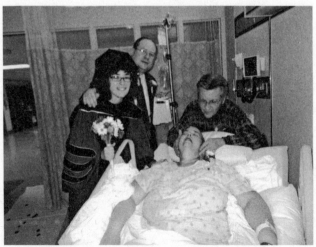

Our wedding day at Ball Memorial.

When it was time to exchange rings, Dad gently propped Mom up so she could see. I could feel her grinning as Rob slipped her ring on me. It was so big I had to press my middle finger and pinky against the sides to hold the gemstones upright. I looked over at Mom with wide eyes and a smile. The chaplain pronounced us husband and wife.

We had eaten cake and changed back into our clothes when Mom moaned. As we looked over, she pulled the oxygen tubes from her face and said, "I'm ready." We didn't object; we had prepared ourselves for this. We gathered around her. Soon she slipped into a coma. The doctors told us she could survive in her current state for up to thirty days.

THIRTY-ONE

No one knew for sure if Mom could hear us in her comatose state. The nurses encouraged us to talk to her, even if we were just narrating our actions, in case she possessed a consciousness we couldn't perceive. And so I talked. And talked and talked.

"Dad's gone home to feed the donkeys, but I'm still here."

"The nurses are here to help roll you."

"Rob stepped out and Dad ran home."

She never gave any indication she could hear or understand me, but I talked all the same. The truth was that I had no idea what else to do. I wasn't going back to work with her death so imminent. I vaguely recall a phone conversation with my department chair in which I said I didn't know when I would return. Normally, I would have felt guilty for bailing on my job for so long, but my emotions were all used up at that point, and I couldn't spare any for my students or colleagues. Rob, I sent home. Though I knew without asking he would stay as long as I needed, there wasn't much point in two of us risking our jobs. When we hugged goodbye in Mom's room, I could tell he wasn't sure Dad and I were in a place to deal with what was coming. But I wasn't uncomfortable with facing my mother's death alone. Alone is how I preferred to face most things.

During those long hours, Dad and I were trying to take care of everything we could think of before Mom died and I would have to leave. Mostly, we needed to get him set up to handle their finances on his own. Mom had been reluctant to hand over the usernames and passwords for their various online accounts, but eventually Dad convinced her to write down what she could remember in a small notebook he had been carrying in his coat pocket. Now I was in charge of logging into each account and resetting permissions and privacy settings so that he could pay the bills for the first time in about twenty years.

Only, it wasn't that easy. Under the heavy influence of narcotics, Mom had transposed many of the login IDs and their passwords.

"Dad went downstairs to get the notebook; he forgot it in the car," I told her from beside her bed. "He wants me to try to get into your Forum account." I kept a list of institutions I would have to call when I had a free moment outside of the hospital. When I opened Mom's laptop, her Facebook account popped up.

"Oh, Mom, you left your Facebook open. I'm going to look through your photos."

My father's voice suddenly filled the room: "Axton! She's awake!"

From my vantage point I could only see her feet, so as quickly as I could, I placed the laptop on the dialysis chair and spun my body around to see Mom's face. Her eyes were round and wide, an urgency swelled behind them. She moved her head and parted her white, dry lips.

"What is it, Pam?" my father pleaded, moving forward toward her with both arms out. "What do you need?"

We watched helplessly as my mother's whole body struggled to produce sound, some last words or dying wish. She shook her head. She couldn't do it.

Seemingly all at once, her eyes dimmed and her jaw loosened. A sigh left her body that sounded like no other breath I have heard before or since. It was her last.

The finality was immediate. We didn't protest, didn't scream or lay our bodies over her. Dad arrived at her bedside and gently closed her eyes with the tip of his finger.

"I guess I should get the nurses," he said. I nodded.

Alone with my mother's body, I sat still and quiet. Grief waited like horses locked in a starting gate.

THIRTY-TWO

MOM WANTED HER BODY donated to science. No obituary, no funeral, no evidence of her earthly life, it seemed. But when the people from the IU School of Medicine arrived, they told us that the chemo and radiation had destroyed Mom's body so entirely it couldn't even be used for research. We needed to make alternate arrangements, they said. While we scrambled to figure out a cremation (her second choice, she had said), my mother's body lay in the hospital room for what seemed like hours, shielded from view by a drab green curtain.

The hospice nurses said we could stay as long as we wanted, but ushered us into a lounge when it was time to zip Mom into the black cocoon of plastic. There was orange juice and shortbread cookies, which seemed like artifacts of a different, happier life. They patiently explained how we should dispose of Mom's arsenal of hard-core painkillers. Grind them up, they said, and then mix them with liquid fabric softener. Otherwise, we might find some hungry addicts going through our garbage. We listened carefully to their instructions; it felt nice to be told exactly what to do.

It was still early afternoon when we left the hospital. Dad drove us in Mom's car back to the farm. It was a Tuesday, and I was surprised to see that the world outside was still operating on a normal schedule. As if nothing had changed. Mail carriers were walking their routes, folks pumped gas, and green lights turned yellow and then red and then green again. It occurred to me that the smell of Mom's car—the vague scent of her perfume—should have stirred some emotion in me, but it didn't. My fatigue was unprecedented. I had lost track of its boundaries. I felt like a wrung-out rag left to dry in the sun. I had gotten married and lost my mother in roughly thirty-six hours. The only sentiment I could really pinpoint when I tried was the anticipation of getting into a real bed.

Dad pulled into the farm's short driveway. Icicles adorned the eaves of the wraparound porch Mom had been so in love with. As I emerged into a bitter wind, I heard the unmistakable wail of Jimmy Page's guitar filling up the barn like a helium balloon about to burst. Two of Dad's employees at the store had been taking care of the animals. Apparently, they were enjoying themselves.

I went in the house and Dad bypassed the house for the barn, of course. It was a predictable move. My father was stoic, pragmatic, Midwestern to his core.

I called Rob. He said he was sorry; he asked what he could do. I told him I was fine, just glad it was over. I took an anxiety pill and fell asleep tangled in the sheets of my mother's bed.

* * *

A fairy-tale-princess kind of sleep would not have scratched the surface of my exhaustion, so when I woke up a few hours later,

I decided to check on Dad, despite the remarkable weight of my tired body. I found him in the living room, watching TV. When he saw me up and about, he wasted no time.

"You need to start going through your mom's things. Take whatever you want. Whatever you don't take is going to the auction, or in the trash."

I felt my eyes widen. Mom had been dead for eight hours.

"Uh, o—kay." This felt bizarre, but I wasn't up for an argument about it.

"I called Lisa. I figure she's about the same size as your mom. She's going to come out tomorrow and go through your mom's closet, so be sure you get anything out of there you want first." He was gesticulating with the remote.

"I'll start in Mom's bathroom," I said, thinking that I could tackle the tiny room in less than an hour. I spun on my heels and headed that way. Dad followed a few minutes later with trash bags and a box for me to put the things I wanted in.

I always knew Mom was a pack rat, but I had never quite understood the extent of it until the days after her death. The bathroom was so petite it should have been manageable, but more than two trash bags in, I felt like I hadn't made a dent. I deposited unused makeup, unopened tampons, and a bag of razors in my to-keep box. I avoided looking at myself in the mirror, at my blotchy skin and sagging eyelids. I wondered if this was how Mom felt when she cleaned out her own mother's things, nearly thirty-five years earlier.

At the very top of the long, narrow cabinet in the corner by the shower, I found bottles of antibiotics and cough syrup that had expired several years earlier. As I reached into the back corner, something odd caught my eye. They looked like thermometers, three of them, stacked carefully atop one another. I stood on my toes and gathered them into my hands like matchsticks.

They were not thermometers. They were pregnancy tests. They were *used* pregnancy tests.

"Jesus!" I yelled when I realized what I was holding. I flung them into an open garbage bag. I knew Mom was still pre-menopausal but I had no idea she and Dad were worried about getting pregnant. I suddenly felt like I needed a hazmat suit to finish clearing out the bathroom.

I slumped down against the wall. My grieving had hardly started and I already felt like I was doing it wrong. The next day, as we sorted through Mom's old blouses, Aunt Lisa would lean in close and ask, "Are you sure about this?" I would say I was, even though I was a long way from certain. I had no idea what I was doing.

My father lived by the seasons, feeding regimens, produce delivery, and inventory schedules. It made sense that he wanted to manifest his heartache into a checklist, something that could be organized, accomplished, and therefore overcome. I just didn't know if I could do it with him.

That night, I returned to my mother's bed. The room was icy. The HVAC system was shot and we would later discover that the house's ancient ducts had long since collapsed. I checked the area around the space heater to be sure I hadn't moved or dropped anything flammable near it. Satisfied, I climbed beneath the heavy bedspread.

Hours later I awoke with the tingle of sweat along my hairline. I was shivering. *Oh God, I've caught the flu from being in the hospital*, I thought. The early-morning darkness and my delirium lifted and I saw that the ceiling fan was spinning so hard it was rocking back and forth from its base. *Mom*—I shook my head as if to dispel the thought. But hadn't I fallen asleep to the lone ticking of the heater?

I stood up and pulled the fan's cord. It took more effort than usual.

In the morning I found Dad in the laundry room, removing his coveralls. The chill of the dawn radiated from his skin.

"Did you turn the fan on in Mom's room?"

"No, it's cold enough in there."

I was about to tell him about my midnight haunting when I saw the tears in his eyes.

"You okay?"

"Yeah," he said, peeling off his boots. "It's just, I'm out there in the barn like it's any other day and your mom's lying in the morgue." His arm pointed in the direction of Albany, to the Meacham Funeral Service mortuary, where Mom's body waited to be taken to the crematory in Fort Wayne.

"Well. What else are you supposed to do, Dad?" I said.

It would be the first Valentine's Day in forty-four years that he didn't spend with Mom. Instead, on this Valentine's Day, her body would be burned to ashes. Together we made breakfast until it was time to get back to our to-do lists.

THIRTY-THREE

WHEN THE PHONE RANG, I knew it was Dad. He had been calling me multiple times a day, to see if I wanted a certain one of Mom's belongings or to tell me about something notable he had found. I didn't mind the interruptions—they let me know he was still upright and functioning.

We had picked up the ashes on the Friday after Mom's death. I strapped them into the front seat on Saturday morning and drove the four hours back to Charleston. I wanted to stay and help out for longer, but I also needed to get back to my job in Illinois.

It had been thirteen days since Mom had died. It had also been fifteen days since Rob and I had gotten married, but that wasn't something we were keeping track of, given everything else. I expected a lonesome tone from my father, maybe even morose—but I did not expect anger. He didn't even say hello; he just started right in:

"What in the *hell* were you thinking, running up a credit card over the limit back in 2001?"

"What? I didn't!" I said, caught off guard. "What are you talking about?" It was early evening and I suddenly realized the apartment had grown dark during my grading. I walked from room to room, switching on lights.

"Don't you lie to me, Axton. I have the statement right here in my hand." I could suddenly picture him, standing in the dimly lit, freezing cold outbuilding, waving a piece of paper around, his hooded sweatshirt and Carhartt coat bundled tightly.

"What credit card company is it?" I asked.

"First USA."

"Dad, that was one of the cards that got taken out in my name as part of the identity theft," I said patiently, tamping down my own frustration and confusion. "What was Mom doing with that?" There was a pause as Dad considered this.

"Well, I don't know why she has it," he said, the fight going out of him. "It's in a file folder out here in the building with your birth certificate."

My blood ran cold. It was as if my body understood something that my mind hadn't yet grasped. I instinctively looked at the closet where I knew my birth certificate was, tucked inside a folder with all my other vital documents. My academic training kicked in.

"Set everything aside, Dad," I said evenly, struggling to maintain my composure. He must have heard it in my voice, because he didn't argue. He just promised he wouldn't throw anything away until I got there.

"Not one thing, okay?" I confirmed.

"Okay. Not anything."

My every instinct told me to immediately walk out of my house, get in my car, and drive until I reached the farm and the papers my dad had found. But I couldn't miss any more work, which meant I had to wait until spring break, a couple of weeks later, to get back to Indiana.

Some small part of me was grateful for the delay, that I could avoid the inevitability of what I already knew was true.

* * *

I was a very sick baby. My hapless parents would watch from the window of the NICU observation room as I, golden with jaundice, threw up every ounce of formula I was fed. During the night, my heart monitor would alert the nurses each time I stopped breathing in my sleep. I had been three weeks late (Mom couldn't be induced because she had preeclampsia) and then I spent another three weeks in the hospital. All of this was decidedly not according to plan.

Mom had been ambivalent about a baby in the first place. She wanted to be a career woman, to make money and a name for herself. For much of their young marriage, my parents didn't plan on children. Their first home was in Portland's Golden Age Village retirement community, where children were not welcome for more than an afternoon. They designed their mobile home without kids in mind. But my father, having raised his sister, was nagged by a desire to raise his own children.

Dad believes now that Mom got pregnant out of fear that she might lose him if they didn't start a family. She was twenty-five and he was twenty-seven when I was born, almost a month after my due date. The pregnancy had been hard and the labor even harder. In the recovery room, Mom told Dad that if he wanted more kids, he "would have to find another woman to have them with." She was done.

I was named after Afton Cooper, the money-loving lounge singer from *Dallas*. Mom wanted to name me Elliott, to honor her parents, but they called me Axton Elliott as a compromise— not Afton, thinking the "f" sound was too soft for the strong, successful child they hoped to raise.

Mom and me, 1982.

Before the hospital sent me home, a nurse pulled Dad aside. "That baby is allergic to milk," she said. "Go down to Indy and get some soy formula at the Children's Palace—she'll be just fine with that." In rural Indiana in the early eighties, soy was still a cosmopolitan ingredient.

So with my special soy formula and my very own heart monitor, my parents took me home to their adults-only mobile home in Portland, on Grandpa Elliott's farm. Although Mom had planned to get back to work right away, she couldn't find anyone who would care for a baby who, at any time and without warning, might stop breathing. Even Grandpa Elliott was too frightened to be alone with me. At age seventy-one, what if the monitor sounded and he couldn't move fast enough to help me? So my mother, who had likely never wanted to be a mother, was trapped in a Holly Park single-wide with a disabled baby for more than seven months.

My health eventually improved but my milk allergy lingered.

(I learned something essential about the unfairness of life by watching other children eat ice cream.) When it was time for grade school, my parents began sending along a juice box, even though the school mandated that I at least take a milk with my cafeteria lunch. Every morning I'd raffle off that day's milk, letting the lucky winner decide if they wanted white or chocolate. This was the routine for three grades, until Mrs. Locker seemingly decided I was getting special treatment. No one else was allowed to bring juice from home, so why was I? I was sent home with a letter, demanding proof.

Mom didn't say anything when I handed her the note from school. She was sitting in Dad's red La-Z-Boy; light cut in through the delicate curtains facing Grandpa's house. I had thought this would be a simple matter of making an appointment with Dr. Burt and acquiring the requisite paperwork, but as I watched my mother's cheeks blush with anger, I felt silly for thinking so.

With her hands on my shoulders, Mom marched me to Grandpa Elliott's kitchen.

"Sit down," she ordered me. I did as I was told. I heard Grandpa shift in his recliner a room away.

Mom opened the fridge and pulled out the half gallon of whole milk. She slammed a glass on the counter.

"Drink it," she said, after she had put the frothy serving in front of me.

"No! I'll get sick!" I screamed.

"Goddammit, Axton. Drink it!" she snarled.

I clamped my jaw shut and looked at the microwave clock: 3:30. Dad would be home by 4:00. He'd rescue me. *Just keep your mouth closed*, I thought to myself. Just then Grandpa appeared behind the counter.

"Pam, don't make her drink that. What are you doing?"

"They want proof she's got a milk allergy, I'll give them proof," she said, as she crossed her arms, eyes full of venom. "Axton, drink it."

I stared at the short glass filled with white poison as I kept my jaw clamped. It was 3:50—not much longer until I would be rescued.

"DRINK THE DAMN MILK!"

Grandpa and Mom argued back and forth. Grandpa told Mom to take me to a doctor if the school needed proof and Mom said something about how backward everyone in Portland was, how the Jay School Corporation was so shitty. After a while they seemed to forget I was there.

A few merciful minutes before 4:00, Dad's truck tires pushed through the loose gravel of the driveway. Through the window I heard him open and close the mobile home's aluminum door. When his footsteps approached the house, I loosened my jaw with relief.

"What in the *hell* is going on in here?" he said, already half-irate by the sight of the milk in front of me. He grabbed the glass from the table and was soon in front of the sink, pouring the milk down the drain. "Go home, Axton."

He didn't have to say it again. I was out the back door before I heard the grown-ups exchange another tense word.

Dad called the school the next day and no one bothered me about my juice box again. But the episode stayed with me. I had learned that my mother would do just about anything to contend with the perceived slights of the world. She would even cause me pain.

PART III

THIRTY-FOUR

IN THE INDECISIVE CHILL of an Indiana spring, I stood in a partially burned outbuilding on my parents' property, surrounded by my mother's papers and documents.

The fire had been electrical. That's what the fire department said. The building had been a chicken coop before the previous owner tried to convert it into a living space. Apparently, the renovation had been slapdash and the wiring caught fire one day a year before while Dad was out feeding the animals and Mom was home doing not much at all. Dad had tried to put it out with a hose, but Mom ultimately called 911. In the end, one wall was burned badly and the rest of the structure sustained water damage. The air remained thick with the smell of smoke, even now. Mom and Dad had been using the space as storage. My mother lost a lot of her documents in the fire, but the papers that remained—the ones that had been under our noses for years—were now spread out on a peeling workbench, telling a story my father did not want to hear.

The outbuilding after fire partially destroyed it.

"I know something's not right. I just don't think we can blame it on your mother," he said, holding fast.

"Dad," I said flatly. "Mom did this."

Everything we had found in the outbuilding told me it was true. It was here, surrounded by fire-scarred walls, dust mites floating in the stale air, that our twenty-year quest for the truth was finally ending. I could not have invented a better metaphor if I tried.

I picked up the credit card statement that my dad had called me about. In addition to the First USA logo, the statement also featured an Edward Jones emblem.

"The only way someone could have opened this card," I said, "was by walking into an Edward Jones branch and applying for it." I locked eyes with my dad. I could tell he was thinking about the years Mom went to work every day at Edward Jones in Albany. "Mom did this on the clock. And she probably made a commission off it, too."

My dad sighed and his shoulders slumped in defeat. He looked around the room at the papers fanned out on display. My mother had been dead for barely a month. She was responsible for the financial turmoil, embarrassment, and fear we'd suffered for twenty years.

The afternoon light slanted through the sooty windows and burned-out gaps in the wall as we dug deeper into Mom's records.

There were dozens of credit card rejection letters.

There was a receipt from EZ Pawn where Mom had taken out a loan on the laptop she had been using for school.

She had taken out another loan from a payday lender in the amount of $300. The loan had an interest rate of 521%.

There was a home inspection document for a property in Muncie, and a contract that had been signed by the real estate agent and the owner. The only signature line that was blank was Mom's. She had gone through the entire process only to back out at the last minute, it seemed.

A stack of recent pay stubs in Mom's maiden name.

A rejection letter for a bank account in Dad's name that Mom had tried to open in Wisconsin.

The larger picture of who I was, and who we were as a family, was fast becoming distorted and unrecognizable. As I zeroed in on each symbolic pixel of that picture—our cell phone, our home, my parents' marriage, the very names we went by, all the times Mom had criticized my appearance, all the times she'd explained away the latest evasion of the identity thief or insisted it wasn't personal—as I considered all of this, what had from afar seemed, if not sentimental, then at least certain, felt grotesque. For years I had struggled with the fact that someone has stolen my identity. But now

I'd been given it back, rotten and ruined. I didn't know if I wanted it anymore.

"Can you believe this?" Dad kept saying on that cold afternoon in March, moving through paper after paper, one mean shock after another.

"I can't," I told him, but the more upsetting truth was that I was beginning to.

THIRTY-FIVE

IN THE INTERVENING WEEKS between Mom's death and our unthinkable discovery, there were indications that something was amiss. On their own, these hints were confusing and incompatible with the woman we knew. But in hindsight—and together with the paperwork in the outbuilding—they had begun to weave the disturbing tapestry of who my mother was when Dad and I weren't around.

Dad's surprises came first. The afternoon after Mom had died, he called the propane company to change the name on the account and to order a refill of heating gas; the tank had dwindled down to 5 percent during the long days we spent sequestered in the hospital. A few hours after we arrived home, I walked into the kitchen to find Dad growling into the phone.

"If you don't come out and refill this tank, I swear I'll pull it out of the ground with my tractor and you'll find it in the middle of 800 South!" There was a heavy silence before Dad snapped again: "Oh, I *can't* do that? I guarantee you I *can*."

"What was that about?" I asked, filling a glass with water.

"They won't sell us propane! Because your mother's name

is on the account. And apparently we owe them nine hundred dollars."

"What?" I set my glass down to cross my arms.

"Yeah, and apparently this has been going on for years. They said your mom would let our bill go into default all spring and summer, and then pay the bill when we needed a refill."

"Why would she do that?"

"I don't know. I gave her the money to pay for it. Every year—I gave her that money."

"Wow." I didn't know what else to say. I guess money had been tighter than I thought.

Dad would fix the problem like he always did—by finding someone who knew him, who knew he was a stand-up guy, who could do him a favor. It's how he managed to patch things up with the electric and gas companies, too. These financial indiscretions made me think of the log-in information Mom had given to us for her various email and online banking accounts and how none of them matched. I was still trying to put together the right combinations by trial and error. But what I assumed was a morphine-induced mix-up may have actually been one last strategic bit of chicanery, my mother buying time before we found out about her bad behavior.

These reckless decisions seemed shitty, to be sure, but not sinister. Just like the inconceivable number of shoes we had found hidden under Mom's bed. Forty pairs, we counted, most of them shiny high heels and hardly worn, if at all. Dad said he had no idea that Mom was buying this stuff. We found jewelry, too, her old weakness, just like my grandmother's. Mountains of beads and baubles, bought with money meant to heat the house.

* * *

It was after dark the next Thursday night when I realized that Dad and I had done very little work to let the world at large know Mom was dead. We had called Aunt Lisa. Dad's employees and coworkers knew, as did the neighbors. But what about Mom's graduate school classmates, her colleagues, all those people she shared a booth with at the diner? I had been preparing lecture notes for a class the next morning when I thought of those people posting unacknowledged messages of encouragement and support on Mom's Facebook wall. I was not connected with her on social media, but I had seen her, on the couch or in her hospital bed, scrolling through her feed enough to know she had been very active on Facebook and open about her illness there.

Using the email address that I had access to, I managed to change the password to her account. Once I was in, I posted a public message for her friends to see:

Hi everyone: this is Pam's daughter, Axton. Judging by the number of messages my mom has received over the past couple of days, it's apparent many of you on her friends list don't realize she lost her battle with Burkitt's Lymphoblastic Leukemia in February. Please message me if you need anything or have any questions.

I reread my post a few times and was about to get back to work when one of Mom's old friends from the radio station messaged me to share his condolences. When I opened the dialogue to thank him, I was able to see the inbox of all my mother's messages. I'm not sure what made me want to scroll through them; maybe I just missed her and wanted to read words she had written, to hear her voice in my head. I clicked on a long conversation Mom was having with a woman I recognized as a friend from the diner in Albany. I scrolled to the top. I scanned at first, not quite sure what I was looking for. A sentence caught my eye:

> *The farmer is concerned about me driving to Richmond every day . . . worried about my safety. He's retired. He can drive me.*

My father was decidedly not retired, still beating a well-worn trail from the barn to work and back again. I wondered what kind of shenanigans my mother was pulling on this lady. I read on.

> *Well . . . I kind of like the cozy stuff we do together. I get dinner, but it's the other stuff I get that I like. LOL!*

I winced. My mother could be so bawdy. I thought about the pregnancy tests I found. My mind told me to close the browser but my finger stayed perched on the down arrow. The messages got weirder.

> *I sure as hell wouldn't want someone to talk to my daughter about my relationships. That's my job and I'll do it when I see fit . . . if I see fit!*
>
> . . .
>
> *Divorce is final. No we're not living together but we're together a lot. I have to move by the end of May and I'm looking at a house, but he wants me to rent or hold off doing anything until May.*
>
> . . .
>
> *I looked at a house today. Other than fuchsia-colored walls in the bedroom, it's ready to move in.*
>
> . . .
>
> *I also know that me still living in that house with John showing up every whipstitch to do his work bothers him a lot more than he lets*

on because he mentions it quite a bit. Casually asks if I've seen "my old man" recently. I tell him he's no LONGER my "old man" and he says, "You were married for 37 years. He's always going to be your old man." I said, "Well you were married for the same amount of time, does it work that way with YOUR divorce?" He said not and I'm sure it doesn't, but he's concerned.

...

I understand where the farmer is coming from on the keeping things quiet for now so I'm giving him some leeway. We're seeing each other, just not so anyone would notice.

I recoiled in horror. That old farmer at the diner? Surely Mom wasn't sleeping with that guy. And what were these bizarre lies about divorcing my dad? Is this why the account was in her maiden name? I looked at the clock; more than an hour had passed since I logged in. I didn't know why my mother was playing her friends like this, but really it was none of my business. I should just close this laptop, I thought, over and over, as I opened a new conversation with another of my mom's friends from Albany.

Nothing is going to happen soon. My daughter is coming for Christmas Eve and Christmas with me and hopefully we can work it out so she can reconnect with him. She knows him. Likes him. Just doesn't know how close we are.

...

He proposed to me and gave me a HUGE diamond ring.
The ring is 4 carats.

I froze. The ring. The HUGE diamond ring. I had used it during my wedding as a stand-in for Mom's real wedding ring, the one we couldn't find. In front of her—in front of my *father*—while she watched me and smiled. My stomach turned over like a derailed train.

Axton is OK with it as she likes him, but it is foreign territory for her.

I thought of the last moments she was alive. As I narrated my movements, the tasks I was checking off. *I'm in this account; I'm in that account. Dad went down to the car to get the notebook with the login information. Oh, Mom, you left your Facebook open. I'm going to look through your photos.* She had sat straight up, with panicked eyes and searching lips. And then, the doctors noted on her death certificate, she died of a heart attack.

Did she realize what I was about to find in her account? Did I kill my mother?

Suddenly it was 3:00 a.m. Maybe I was delirious. Maybe I was dreaming. The messages got stranger:

I went out for a fast run about 6 a.m. No one much on the lake but fishermen near the shore so I can speed. Was just rounding the last speed zone and they came out on the other side of an island right in front of me . . . looking behind them and I was running about 85. I threw the boat in reverse as soon as I saw them and turned hard left. I missed them but they flipped the jet ski and hit her in the head and killed her. They'd stolen it. I dropped anchor and grabbed all my life jackets and went over the side. I saved him but she was gone before I got there.

Fortunately there were a lot of witnesses. Police say I'm some kind of hero, but I sure don't feel like one. She was in foster care and a ward of the state of Ohio. He's 16 and his parents lost both their jobs and have lost everything. They're afraid I'm going to sue them.

No one can sue me because they got hurt committing a crime. The farmer was BESIDE himself Friday night when I got home. I didn't tell him until I was about halfway home. Steve's sister and brother brought me home and he told them to bring me straight to him and bypass my place. He may be an SOB in public, but he's the most amazing boyfriend in private!

I turned to the right and looked at my mother's urn, sitting on a shelf on my living room. "What the fuck?!" My knuckles sang with pain as I punched its brass exterior.

The first day John left me home alone with Axton was the worst day of my life.

Maybe she was jealous Dad got to leave the house, or maybe she resented me for being her anchor there. But reading those words—that the worst day of my mother's life was one she spent at home with me—was a new kind of hurt, more painful than the identity theft, and certainly more devastating than watching Mom be ravaged by cancer.

After I sent out an email canceling class, I called Rob at work. I'm sure I sounded deranged, spitting out fragments of these preposterous stories, trying to make him understand things I couldn't even articulate because they were so bizarre.

"Just leave it alone. You don't know what it means—don't tell your dad and just leave it alone."

"What kind of sick games was she playing with her friends?" I repeated.

A few weeks later, I would learn Mom was playing sick games with everyone—including me.

THIRTY-SIX

WE FOUND COLLECTION LETTERS in old shoeboxes; we found shut-off notices shoved in between the yellowed pages of dusty books. We found pawn shop receipts at the bottom of forgotten tote bags. We found more paperwork about the house with the fuchsia walls. We found a $400 receipt for a *2 pc CZ ring set* from a local department store. My cubic zirconia wedding rings—from my mother's man on the side—which she apparently bought *herself* at the Muncie Meijer.

We were taking hits from all sides. There was no time to be sad, and our mourning seemed to stop dead in its tracks. How do you grieve for someone you clearly didn't know? When I had time to think about anything other than damage control, I would remember the moments I cried about the identity theft with my mother, when I had called sobbing on my couch in West Lafayette or after walking all over Havana begging someone to approve me for an auto loan. I thought of the empty cupboards in the kitchen and the day the sheriff showed up to haul Mom to jail and the way the bursar's office smelled like moldy boxes of paper and how cold I was doing my homework on the patio in December. I thought about all of the incredulous faces I had looked into, while explaining that I wasn't a deadbeat, wasn't a ne'er-do-well, but rather a helpless victim. I thought about how I had at first felt unworthy of my fiancé's affection because my family was so screwed up. I thought about—and ached for— that awkward thirteen-year-old girl at school camp, feeling like I was going to die because the terror of my parents' trouble had found its way into my blood cells. *I don't know why you take this so personally; it's not personal,* she always said. I couldn't think of anything more personal than how my mother's deceit had stunted our life and splintered my being.

But there was more. Now that she was gone and unable to protect her house of cards or to throw us off the trail that would lead us to it, things started to fall apart in alarming ways.

The first sign that there was a problem with the taxes were the license plates. Mom had died with a pending registration renewal due in two days on the Chevy Lumina Rob had given her when she totaled Dad's car three years earlier. The plates on the Park Avenue, Town Car, and truck were due as well on Valentine's Day. Renewing them was high on Dad's to-do list, but he needed my help to do it online; the computer was not his strong suit. Together, we went to the library in Portland with Mom's laptop in tow, and took a table in the back of the library. Dad had his paperwork and a debit card in front of him on the table, like a studious pupil, observing carefully as I navigated the BMV's website. He would need to learn to do this on his own soon.

"That's weird," I said, after the system rejected my attempt a second time. "It says these plates can't be renewed online."

My father sighed.

"Why don't we just go down to the license branch in Albany and do it in person?" I said, hoping to buoy his spirits.

"That's fine. I need to get a duplicate title for the truck anyway. Your mom said the BMV screwed up and sent a title but it got lost in the mail, but who knows."

I braced myself for another cruel surprise.

"The bank has the title for your truck, sir," said the gray-haired lady behind the counter at the BMV. Her eyes conveyed a familiar message: *Oh, here we go.*

"That can't be right. That loan was paid off years ago." I could tell my father was gearing up for another fight.

"Dad, we'll figure this out. Mom probably has paperwork somewhere at home. We'll straighten this all out." I turned my attention back to the woman. "Can we just renew these tags, please? We need to change the name on them, too. I've brought a death certificate." I slid the heap of paperwork across the counter.

After she tapped on her keyboard for a few moments, the woman looked at us with some hesitation. "Were you aware that there are tax liens against a number of your vehicles, sir?"

"What in the *hell*—" My father's eyes were large and searching mine.

"There has to be some mistake," I said, aware that now *I* was singing one of Mom's old refrains.

"No," she said, stretching out the syllable like she was trying to soften the blow. "Looks like you need to catch up on some income tax?"

I was used to this tactic. Customer service people must be trained to speak in questions and not allegations. Despite her rhetorical acrobatics, my father's face was ripening with anger— jaw locked and unblinking eyes.

"You know what? We'll look into this and come back," I said, reclaiming the paperwork, as if we needed to double-check a plate number, not investigate whether we were tax evaders. Mom had driven that truck for so long—surely I would find something that said it was paid off. But in Mom's stack of papers, instead we found documents that showed the truck loan had been extended multiple times since it was purchased in the midnineties. Always without my father's knowledge. What was originally supposed to be a five-year loan still had a balance nearly twenty years later. The title Mom had sworn got lost in the mail? It was never sent.

The income tax mystery proved harder to figure out. While I had discovered delinquent property tax payment transactions in Mom's bank account records, we couldn't locate old returns. Since it was time for Dad to do his taxes anyway, we decided to find a tax preparer who might be able to get him back on track. He asked around the store and got some recommendations for a woman in a small town close to Indianapolis. It was an overcast day in mid-March when Dad loaded his passenger seat with every document he thought might be relevant to his finances.

I wasn't with my father when he met the tax preparer, but I was home when he came back all too quickly, his face pale and panicked.

"Your mom hasn't paid the taxes in thirteen years." The words left him like air from a slashed tire.

"Slow down," I said, sitting motionless in a recliner, where I had been catching up on email. "Tell me everything she said."

"She said, 'You haven't paid taxes in thirteen years, sir. I don't think I can help you,'" he said, exasperated. With me. With the world.

"Right, but what else did she say?"

"That's it. I'm finished. I don't have the money to begin paying it all now."

"Listen—we can fix this. We can get a tax attorney and explain that you didn't know—"

"I'm going to find a home for the animals, and then—and then I think I'll just go." My dad was looking beyond me, as if he could visualize a place far away enough that Mom's bullshit couldn't follow him. Did such a place exist?

"Dad. Stop."

"I'll call you whenever and wherever I figure out what to do next."

"I think Mom has taken enough from you already."

"Well, I'm going to have to sell this place. This is the end of the line."

"No, it's not the end of anything. She has taken enough and I'll be damned if she's going to take the farm, too."

My father remained unconvinced that afternoon, but in the following days I tracked down a tax lawyer based in Florida who specialized in cases like ours. He said he would be happy to help us but would need an up-front payment of nearly $5,000. For a few hours we thought we had hit a dead end until Dad remembered that he had, many years ago when given the opportunity at the store, taken out a $10,000 life insurance policy on my mother.

Using the money he received for my mother's untimely death, my father began the endless, arduous process of paying back her debts. He had finally run out of favors.

THIRTY-SEVEN

MY MOTHER HAD FIVE PO Boxes (that I know about) spread out across the state. The one in Portland and the one in Albany that we were aware of, along with the one on Seventy-First Street in Indianapolis. Mom had acquired it when she worked at Q95, saying it would be more convenient for her to get the mail closer to work. There wasn't a lot in there, just some satellite TV bills and junk mail. At the UPS Store in Muncie, however, we found a trove of disturbing documents.

My dad smoothed the death certificate out on the counter. "We believe my wife had a mailbox here," he said.

The young man leaned over and searched with his index finger for the name. When he landed on *Pam Betz* he jerked his head up, giving Dad a knowing smirk. "Oooh, yeah. She's got a box here all right."

It took two workers to bring out the cartons of overflow mail in my mother's name. Her actual box was so stuffed that when we unlocked it, mail sprung out like one of those prank snakes in a can. Among the envelopes that were scattered across the floor, there were thirteen certified letters from the IRS, the last one indicating the imminent seizure of the house. These documents only represented the last four months of my mother's life, when she was too sick to drive.

I never really made a conscious decision not to go find the mailbox in Geneva, a little town just north of Portland. As it was, I had enough paperwork to make sense of. I also had— though I was in the habit of forgetting about them for days at a time—a job and a weeks-old marriage.

* * *

Between my parents, Rob had always felt my mother was the "normal" one. Mom could talk to anyone about anything, and she and Rob could always carry on a long conversation about golf, TV shows, or music. When she worked at the radio station, Mom had snagged Rob some free Rush tickets—and with them, his loyal affection.

Dad, on the other hand, was pretty clear: if you wanted to talk to him, you could meet him out in the barn. One of the first times I took Rob home, my father shook his head in bemusement as he watched my future husband hitting foam golf balls in our front yard. It was December and it was sleeting; Rob was wearing shorts.

"Come look at your boyfriend, Axton," he said in a tone he usually reserved for things he disapproved of on the evening news.

It was a few weeks after the scene in the outbuilding when I showed up to Rob's house in East Moline. It was the first time we had seen each other since my mother had died—and since we had gotten married. An aging, gray snow covered the back-yard of his suburban ranch-style home. I leaned against the sink, staring at the dainty floral wallpaper—the legacy of the home's previous owner. I fought back the exhaustion that seemed to radiate through my bones. I was as worn down as my tires were becoming from crisscrossing the soggy Midwest.

"I'm telling you, it's true—it was her all along."

"I really don't think your mom was capable of that. Are you sure you have all the pieces to this thing?" I was used to his typical engineerese. "A lot of this stuff could mean anything. What if she had that file because she was disputing the charges on your behalf?"

"How do you explain the taxes? The defaulted accounts? The Facebook messages?"

"I just can't believe it," he said, shaking his head.

In time, Rob did believe it. We all did. And we all internalized it in different ways. My father raged, Rob made his peace, and I—well, I began to feel empowered. I had done what everyone told me could never be done. I solved the case. A twenty-year-old case. And I intended to do with any and all of the information I could track down what I had always done: make it a part of my work. I didn't need Rob to help me, and I didn't ask him to. After years of long-distance, and the lonely struggle of my childhood, it felt unnatural to ask for assistance—logistical, emotional, or otherwise. Rob was there for me, but I didn't need him to be there *with* me.

I can see now that treating my mother's unthinkable sins as if I were a CSI technician and not her only child might have been a bit of a deflection on my part. Academia had long been my therapy, and I was used to transforming the unwieldy and nebulous emotions of my personal life into the cold, hard facts of research. But I can forgive myself for that. Knowledge, I've found, will not betray you the way that people will.

THIRTY-EIGHT

THERE WERE SIXTEEN LONG and eventful years between my uncle Larry's birth and my mother's. I didn't know much about them except what Mom had told me. According to her, my grandma Lelah had left Larry and his brother, Mike, in an orphanage and run away to California, returning to Indiana a few years later to marry my grandfather and subsequently reclaim her children. I knew that Lelah had been young—too young to raise two children while enduring an abusive marriage—and I always figured that's why she had run away: out of fear, desperation, or both. But as I dug deeper into my mother's mysteries, it became apparent I didn't know much about her mother's, either.

I understood that the 1940s were a different time for women in America, but dumping two toddlers in an orphanage—I intuited even as a young girl—must have taken some icy resolve. Mom liked to skip over the part about the orphanage and had begun telling the story as if Lelah had dropped the boys off with their aunt Grace and uncle Smoke. In reality it was Grace and Smoke who'd had to retrieve the children themselves when they were notified the boys had been surrendered.

Larry visited the farm not long after Mom died, to help sort through the mountains of Mom's stuff—Dad was still trying to rid his life of Elliott family memorabilia but Larry hadn't been much help. "It will all be yours again in a few years anyway," he told us.

We were chatting in the living room afterward and I decided to ask Larry about my grandmother.

"What is your first memory of Lelah?"

"She just showed up at the door one day," Larry said.

"Did you know who she was?" my dad asked.

"No. I hadn't seen her in I don't know how long. She goes, 'You don't recognize me, do you?'"

"Did you think Uncle Smoke and Aunt Grace were your parents?" I asked. I couldn't remember how Smoke had earned that nickname, but I vaguely remembered they lived in Fort Wayne.

"I did," Larry said with a nod. "Then Lelah says: 'I'm your mother. I'm here to take you home.' But she had been back in town for a while by then—long enough to meet your grand-father and get married."

"Wait, so she had been back in Indiana for months by the time she got around to finding you? Was she just not going to come and get you?"

"I don't think so. George made her."

"Man, that woman was an obsessive spender," my dad inter-rupted, momentarily lit up with some kind of rueful nostalgia. "Wretched excess."

"What do you mean?" I prodded.

"She bought multiples of everything, for no reason. One time I remember she bought fourteen boxes of Chinese checkers. Just because they were on sale!"

I thought of the shoes under Mom's bed.

"She married George because she thought he had money, you know," he continued. "Boy, she was disappointed."

My father and my uncle shared a laugh. As if he knew what I was thinking, Larry said, "I guess your mom was more like our mom than I thought. All this crazy stuff you've been telling me kind of proves that." Outside, the sky turned purple; I could hear the goats bleating to one another.

"What do you know about my mom's last year in high school, the year she spent at Indian Lake, Larry?"

Larry looked up at the ceiling, thought for a moment. "I remember they had horrible fights about that. Pam wanted to get out of Portland so bad, said everyone was mean to her because of George's beer business."

"Wait!" I interjected. "I thought George and Lelah *wanted* Mom to go live over there. To get away from Dad."

"No, no, no. Pam begged and begged for them to let her live there that year. Of course, George thought that was crazy— she was way too young to be living by herself. I was around for some of the big fights about it. But Pam got her way."

"But the restraining order?" I looked at my dad.

"Oh, I bet she told them he was harassing her or stalking her or something," Larry answered for him. "That's probably how she ended up winning that battle."

My father pursed his lips and nodded.

"So manipulative," I said.

"Just like her mother," my dad echoed.

"Michelle told me she remembered Lelah lying on the couch, dying of cancer, with a full face of makeup, hair done up like she was going to a gala," I told my uncle. "That's my mother to a T."

"Oh that was the least of it. Lelah was good at appearances—won the Home of the Month and all that. Everyone thought she and George were so perfect. But they never ate dinner together, went to different churches, drove everywhere separately."

"I never saw them exchange affection," Dad chimed in.

"They had their own lives. It's easy to get away with things when no one's watching."

I observed my father. His rabbit-gray hair feathered behind his ears where glasses hugged his olive skin. I wondered what I didn't know about my parents' marriage. I wondered if Dad had been watching her. I wondered if my mother would have come back for me.

THIRTY-NINE

MAYBE NOT ALL KIDS GROW UP thinking their parents' love is special, immutable, but I certainly did. Although I had been witness to some of their most explosive fights, I had always imagined them dying hand in hand, bound together for eternity. They had made it through so much; surely, I had thought, there was a profound connection at the core of their union.

"Oh, I wanted nothing to do with your mom," my dad said when I asked him to tell me again about how they met. We were on the phone a state away, a few days after our conversation with Larry. I realized that Mom was the only one who ever spoke of their courtship. I told Dad I needed the unpolished version, to hold nothing back.

My parents met—at the behest of Aunt Patty—at a roller rink in Fort Recovery, Ohio. The scene of two important battles of the Indian Wars, the streets of the town are lined with cannonballs and American flags, like a perpetual Independence Day. Dad spent a lot of time at the roller rink when he was a kid, when he wasn't scraping together money doing odd jobs on area farms. Aunt Patty told him about my mother: "a cute little girl from Portland" she thought he would like. My mother was twelve and already quite boy crazy.

Dad spent that first night at the rink trying to get away from my mom. But they would meet again at a Christmas party where their friends dressed Dad up as Santa Claus so that my mother would have an excuse to sit on his lap. Dad doesn't remember the moment his annoyance melted into affection, but it may have been around the time Mom offered to do things with him any fourteen-year-old boy would have a hard time resisting. Soon they were together every day, and my dad gradually ingratiated himself into the family.

"Your mom was fun, and outgoing, and I liked delivering beer to the taverns. I liked being part of a family." Beer and sex. What teenage boy could resist? When I asked him why he married her, my dad said, "I had everything I wanted. Why wouldn't I marry her?"

It's hard to know what my mother's motives were in marrying my father. She had just spent a year away from Dad in Indian Lake under the guise that her parents didn't want her near him, but now it seemed likely that she had only been itching for her freedom. Dad has always thought she was two-timing him that year at the lake, and, given Mom's propensity for affairs, this seemed more likely than not.

Still, my father was happy, and he wanted a family, so he married her. "A lot of people told me not to," he said. "Told me this or that about her, that she thought she was better than everyone else or just using me. My family couldn't stand her, but mostly because she took me away from them."

My mother had not included that detail in her account of the engagement.

My father reported that the years before I arrived were steady, and mostly happy. They moved to the farm to take care of Grandma, but then Grandma died. Mom wanted to stay to take care of Grandpa Elliott, so Dad learned to manage a small farm, and eventually he convinced her to give motherhood a go.

"I think she did it to ensure the marriage more than any-thing," he said. At this point, we didn't have to dance around the fact that Mom didn't want a child and probably never should have had one.

"And after you, she got mean. She changed. I didn't even like to leave you alone with her. When I would come home from work, she'd meet me at the door and say, 'Take her,' and thrust you into my arms."

I immediately thought of all those hours Mom spent mind-lessly watching soap operas when I was in preschool, scolding me fiercely if I changed the channel to watch cartoons. I thought of how she never wanted to sit on the floor and play with me, and how instead I just played with the cats. I wondered if that's why Dad took me everywhere he could, building trails in the woods, feeding the donkeys in the evening, or baling hay in the miserable heat.

"There was no satisfying her, no matter what I did. She hated the farm, she hated Portland, but she wouldn't leave."

A profound sadness settled in my chest. Had my parents' marriage been a miserable farce? "But you were happy, right? Sometimes?"

My father was quiet for a moment. Even from afar, I could sense his discomfort.

"Axton, do you remember when you were in the second grade, I picked you up from school, and you told me about all the kids whose parents had different last names? You were worried that was going to happen to us. I told you then—and

I meant it—that if I had any say, we would never get divorced. And so we didn't."

"After you left for college, you know, I stopped doing as much on the farm. Your mom wanted no part in it; she just wanted me to be busy. Hand her money and stay busy. I must have given her at least two hundred thousand dollars over the years from the hay and donkeys. I thought it was going right into the retirement account. But we led separate lives at that point. We had long since stopped talking to any of our mutual friends, and it was just easier that way. I'd stay out in the barn until I knew she was asleep, and I'd go to work before she even woke up."

"Did you know about other men?"

"I should have. Once she said she was going on a work trip to Ohio so I decided to check the oil for her, and make sure the spare tire was still good. I opened the trunk and..." He trailed off.

"And?" I said, like I was willing a child to describe a bad dream.

"There were dog collars and chains. Leather straps and an S-and-M book."

"Oh God." I felt my cheeks burning. "Tell me you confronted her."

"I did. And I shouldn't have believed it, but she said Valentine's Day was coming up and she was making a video for me."

I was silent.

"I know, it was stupid. I almost followed her that night, to see where she was going, but then I realized I didn't even care."

This version was radically different from what I had been imagining while I was away chasing degrees. I had so wrongly interpreted the disintegration of their relationship as the kind of assured companionship older people settle into after their kids have gone. A quiet but grounding love.

"Was she there every night, though, at the end? Or was she staying over with her farmer friend?" I winced at the nickname. But I had given my dad the Facebook messages so he could read them for himself.

"She was always here. Maybe she got home late, but she always came home."

"And you never suspected it was her behind the identity theft?"

"Your mother had a bad temper and she was extremely manipulative. But I never thought she was capable of doing these kinds of things. I spent forty-six years with her. It's unbelievable, Axton. Unbelievable."

I couldn't figure it out—why did Mom do this? My father wasn't dumb. He had built a working—and profitable—hobby farm from scratch. Taught himself to breed and care for some of the most sought-after livestock and hay in the region. Customers and employees at the store adored him. I knew firsthand how domineering Mom could be, how stupid she could make you feel for questioning her. I understood how my mother could pull this off. I just didn't understand why she would.

FORTY

My father was suffering. He tried to hide the emotional toll of my mother's duplicity, but his body betrayed the truth. When his shift at the store would end, when there were no more animals to feed or stalls to clean, his blood pressure would shoot up like a flare gun. At the very moment he willed it to rest, his heart would unleash all of its fury, as if it were just waiting for him to pay attention.

He reluctantly went to the doctor. They put him on blood pressure medicine. It didn't work. So they told him to double the dosage and gave him an additional prescription. That didn't work. Soon the doctors were worried there was some kind of blockage. I was worried, too.

Dad's old friend Joe, a pastor, began to stop by the house frequently to check on him and cajole him into attending services he said might expedite the healing process. Joe even offered to put up a hitching post outside the church so that Dad could ride one of his donkeys there. Dad was always quick to invite Joe in for a chat, but church didn't interest him.

"You'll be together one day," Joe told him. "She's in a good place."

"Joe, you don't know that," Dad would repeat defiantly.

A few nights after I delivered the file folder full of Mom's most indecent Facebook messages, he waited patiently for Joe to stop by. When he did, Dad invited him in, sat him down in an old recliner, and handed Joe the folder. As the wide-eyed pastor sorted through the damning records of adultery and debauchery, Dad asked, "Still think she's in a good place?"

Joe hesitated. "I think she's in a very bad place, in fact."

It was the last time the pastor came by.

* * *

I couldn't ease my father's physical or emotional pain, but I worked nearly every day to sort out his financial trouble. In a bank account in Indianapolis, I found $5,000. When I told my father, he was incredulous. "She said there would be fifty dollars in there," he exclaimed.

"I know, Dad." I sighed heavily. It *was* outrageous. But in comparison to all the lies, this particular transgression felt pretty mild. Plus, we could use the money to pay off some back taxes. So I was surprised when Dad called a few days later with another plan for the money.

"I really want this bike," he said. My father had always wanted a Harley-Davidson motorcycle. Of course, during the nearly two decades of my parents' financial turmoil, a bike just wasn't in the budget. Mom always promised that once she finally got the well-paying job she deserved, a Harley for Dad would be one of her first big purchases. When we found out what Mom had actually been spending her money on, that promise seemed as cruel as it did hollow. But now an acquaintance of one of Dad's employees was offering him a deal. The man was dying of cancer and selling his belongings at ridiculous prices. The orange-and-black, custom Harley Davidson was what my father had been dreaming of for years. And at $8,000, the price was within reach. "This is a stupid decision, financially," he thought out loud.

I understood that my dad was more or less asking my permission.

"It's not the best thing financially," I said, "but it might be the best thing for you right now." I asked him to send me pictures of this dream bike. When I opened the text message attachments, I saw that it wasn't a touring bike, or a Sunday afternoon joyride bike. Not the kind of bike for lovers on a road trip. This was a sport bike. Built for speed. Built for one person.

A few days later, Dad owned a Harley. He started taking it out immediately, zooming down the Indiana back roads like a teenager. When I asked him how he liked it, he said, "When I can't handle things around here, I just *go*." He started attending rallies and concerts at the Harley shop in Marion, meeting new people and distancing himself from his old life, the one in which Mom was his axis.

But Dad couldn't escape all his problem on two wheels. Now completely alone on the farm, my father seemed to age decades in just a few months.

"This house is too big for just me," he would say, beginning to sound like Grandpa Elliott had years ago. If anyone suggested that he wouldn't be alone forever, Dad would object vehemently while shaking his head: "I'm never gonna have another woman, nope, not gonna be taken advantage of again."

It wasn't as if he didn't have options. Almost as soon as Mom died, it seemed every other woman in Jay County wanted to check in on him. Dad was in his late fifties but was always mistaken for being much younger. An attractive, eligible bachelor was quite the commodity in rural Indiana. Dad called these women gold diggers. Never mind there was no gold left.

I was still a newlywed myself when Dad started making comments about what a mistake it had been to get married at all. I tried to not take it personally when he would say, "Why would anybody want to get married? I'll be in charge of my own money and my own things." He also made offhand comments about how he had wasted his life and that after all those years, he had never really known Mom at all. These asides broke my heart, but I knew how he felt. Unlike Mom, my father was not one to emote or dwell on past hurts, but I could tell that the pain of my mother's betrayal fed on him like a parasite, siphoning any happiness from his newfound freedom.

* * *

It was "dead week" at Eastern Illinois University when Dad called. ("Dead" is kind of a misnomer; there's plenty of activity on campus, except it's mainly happening indoors as students and professors gear up for finals week.) I was spending my dead week grading at the kitchen table and when the phone rang, I was annoyed by the distraction. We made small talk for a bit, while I impatiently eyed the stack of papers in front of me. I was about to cut the conversation short when Dad dropped a bomb.

"So, I'm taking someone to meet Aunt Patty," he said sheepishly.

"Who?" He suddenly had my full attention.

"Just a woman from work."

I knew where this was going. "Do you really think that's a

smart idea, Dad? It might be a little soon," I said, my volume and pitch inching higher.

"She's just a friend from work, Axton."

"Dad, I need to go. I have a lot of grading to do." I slammed the phone down on the table. I sat back in the chair and glared into the living room. Mom's urn was gleaming in the late-April sunlight on the bookshelf.

"What the hell am I supposed to do now?" I yelled at her. After a pause, I yelled again: "Why am I even asking you? If it wasn't for you, this wouldn't be happening!"

I went upstairs and called Rob. I told him Dad had a girl-friend. He laughed and laughed.

"Axton. You didn't think this was going to happen? Your dad has been in a relationship since he was fourteen. He's never been alone before."

I figured Rob has a point. It wasn't that I didn't trust my dad's judgment; I just didn't trust anybody's. I waited a few hours before I called him back.

"I told Candice how you reacted," he said. Now she wasn't just a friend. She was *Candice*. And my dad was giving her the details of our private conversations. Rob was right: my father needed a partner as if it was coded into his DNA.

"I'm sorry, Dad. I'm just worried you're going to get taken advantage of again."

Candice was the floral department manager at the store where Dad worked. She had been through her own share of hard times, and a bad marriage had left her as uneager to couple up as Dad. But she was there when he needed to talk, which was often in the weeks before and after Mom's death. At first, he confided in her about the stress associated with Mom's cancer treatments and trying to keep up with the housework, farmwork, and responsibilities at the store, but later he shared his confusion as Mom's crimes revealed themselves one by one. When there seemed to be no bottom to the well of my father's hurt, Candice provided a ledge, somewhere for Dad to rest and yell into the abyss.

Candice wasn't just young (eighteen years younger than Dad); she was *youthful*. She liked going to concerts at the big amphitheater in Noblesville, and she cherished her summer getaways on the Gulf of Mexico. She maintained close relationships with a large extended family. While at first they seemed like opposites, I came to appreciate that Candice was the perfect foil to my father's stoic nature. Like his bike, she denied him his insularity, demanding he venture out into a world that was bigger than Mom, more compassionate than her crimes had made it seem. Perhaps, for my father, their relationship was less about not being alone and more about truly being with someone for the first time in his life.

Still, I worried about my father's vulnerability. Mom had made me wary of everyone, especially anyone trying to get close to Dad. More than anything, I was exhausted. And I wasn't excited about welcoming a stranger into the family.

When the semester was officially over and grades were in the books, I headed back to Indiana to help my father to further empty the house of Mom's stuff. It had been such a dreadful few months for him, I half expected the farm to be buried in weeds and crabgrass. But as I pulled in the driveway, I was surprised to see the flower beds full and vibrant, the front yard trimmed neatly. There was an unfamiliar pickup truck parked by the house, but no sign of Dad's car. My heart sank.

Candice opened the door with a warm smile on her face. Her dark hair was loose and she was wearing housework clothes. "You must be Axton!" she said, looking like she wanted to hug me.

"Hi, Candice. Is my dad home?" I managed a smile but made it clear with my body language that I didn't need a hug.

"No, he's still at work. He thought we could get some of this cleaning done together," she said, waving her hands toward the house behind her. "Come in!" She moved aside for me to enter. *Of course he did*, I thought.

Like the outside of the house, the inside was spotless. The last time I had been in the house it had been falling apart at an alarming rate. Now, fresh paint had begun to replace peeling flower-print wallpaper in the kitchen. Candice had done all this on her own volition, because she wanted to help my dad, because she wanted him to be happy.

After a few awkward moments of small talk in the kitchen, we moved into the laundry room together. In an adjacent closet were piles of old shoes, clothes, and containers of crafting materials. More of Mom's things: there seemed to be no end to it. Candice grabbed a trash bag and offered it, open, to me. "Should we just trash all of this?" she asked. "Your dad said to trash it, if you don't want any of it."

"Maybe," I answered. The piles were overwhelming. Looking at my mother's impractical collection of brightly colored shoes, I thought back to the weeks of my childhood when the refrigerator sat empty except for a few condiments and a jar of pickles, when I was so hungry it hurt.

As those terrible thoughts ricocheted around my head, I felt Candice's presence like a warm light beside me, and suddenly, I understood why my father was willing to take the leap. I realized that I, too, wanted Candice's help. She was like a relief pitcher, coming into the game with new hope and stored-up energy. But could we trust her? Was she really on our side?

I picked up a well-worn sandal and pointed its toe at Candice. "See this? *This* is what she spent it on. Shoes!"

Candice nodded.

"If you're looking for money, you are barking up the wrong tree," I told her, kindly but firmly, still clutching the shoe. "Mom took it all."

"I understand. Your dad has already told me," she said softly.

I tossed the shoe back onto the pile and, silently, we began stuffing much of my mother's belongings into trash bags.

FORTY-ONE

I STAYED IN INDIANA for a while. Normally, I would have gone to Rob's house in Illinois as soon as grades were in the computer, but a thousand unanswered questions pulled me home like a magnet. There were boxes of paperwork to thumb through and endless conversations I needed to have with my father. One of them was about straightening out Mom's unpaid student loans, for her master's degree and the doctorate she had just started on when she was diagnosed with leukemia. As Dad sorted through a stack of torn envelopes at his desk in the den, preparing them for my inspection, I stood over his shoulder, telling him what I had researched about discharging a deceased person's debt. On top of the taxes, a hundred grand in student loan debt—debt that Mom had racked up unbeknownst to Dad—felt like the anvil that would break the camel's back.

"I know it's stressful—I have a lot of student loan debt, too," I said, trying to reassure him.

"How much do you have?" he said absentmindedly, his fingers still moving through old mail.

"A hundred thousand dollars."

He stopped and looked up at me. "That's impossible. We paid for your college."

"Um . . . no. You didn't."

"Yes . . . we did."

A familiar dread crept in between my ribs. I spoke very slowly: "How much money were you giving Mom for my college? Per semester?" My gut told me where this was going.

"Eleven thousand dollars."

"Mom was giving me *three thousand* a semester for my tuition and telling me there wasn't money for the rest. That I had to take out loans for that. You paid my tuition, but loans paid for my housing. Eight thousand a semester."

"I gave your mother money every year for your housing. Every semester." My dad's voice was becoming distant as he began to realize what had already dawned on me.

Mom had stolen $48,000 of money earmarked for my college expenses—plus interest—but for what purpose?

"Thank God I finished school in three years." I remembered how rushed I felt to get through my undergraduate degree, like someone was chasing me. Someone had been chasing me.

I wondered how deep this all went. I wondered when, or if, we would ever find the bottom.

FORTY-TWO

FOR WEEKS I MOVED THROUGH the house like a forensics team, looking for evidence in every possible place my mother might have stashed it. In the back of her closet, I found a collection of old purses. I laid them on the bed and checked them one at a time, frisking each pouch and poking my fingers into every lipstick-shaped pocket. Crumpled receipts were set aside for further examination, and other effects, like old gum or coins, were put into appropriate piles. I wasn't turning up much until, in an old red-and-beige-striped purse, I found a folded-up letter still in its envelope. It was addressed to Grandpa Betz.

My dad's dad didn't live with my parents when Mom died; two years prior he had moved back in with my aunt Lisa. But he had joined them in the move from the farm in Portland to the place in Redkey, trading his mobile home for a room in the house. It would have been crowded except Grandpa pretty much kept to himself. He'd go to one veteran's hall or another each day, and otherwise stay in the living room, watching the Weather Channel or the Channel 13 news. He was so emotionally isolated from the family that once, when he was picked up after bingo for driving under the influence, he forfeited his one phone call from the drunk tank, opting instead to hitchhike back to his car in the morning. When Grandpa pulled in the driveway at 6:30 a.m., my dad was hurriedly feeding the animals so he could head out to scan the county's ditches for a car or a dead body.

Grandpa Betz in 2009.

"Where in the hell have you been?" my dad yelled across the lawn.

"County hotel!" Grandpa snapped back as he slammed the back door.

His driver's license was suspended while he attended mandatory substance abuse counseling. That Christmas he gave us all cards with money inside. It was so out of character that, as he opened the envelope, my father asked, "Are you dying?"

To get behind the wheel again, Grandpa had to buy special car insurance and offer proof of it to the state. He asked my mother to help him with the online forms. This was probably when she was able to glean the personal information she needed to open multiple credit cards in his name. The letter I found in the purse was the first of a few collection notices I would find, for low-limit, high-interest credit cards belonging to one Leonard Betz.

Grandpa Betz wasn't an ideal target. Mom had told me once that he had never established credit and gambled away all the money he ever had. But he was as vulnerable and oblivious as the rest of us, and so Mom used him for the couple thousand dollars he was worth. We chose not to tell him about the identity theft; by the time we figured it out he was dealing with multiple health issues and didn't need any added stress.

At the end of his life, my grandfather suffered through one indignity after another. A twisted intestine landed him in the hospital for weeks. Years of wearing cheap and ill-fitting shoes led to gangrene in his foot. Because he couldn't walk without assistance, Aunt Lisa moved him into a Medicaid facility, where the wall in his room was pocked with shoddy patch jobs; apparently the previous occupant had some anger issues. The last morning I saw him alive, my grandfather fell asleep sitting up, but only after he peppered Dad with questions about the new motorcycle.

"Good for you, Johnny," he told my dad.

Later that day, Dad called to tell me Grandpa had fallen and broken his hip. A couple of weeks later, he died.

He left behind no money for a funeral. Dad was still treading water in the deep end of his tax trouble and Lisa didn't have extra money for one. Lisa sold Grandpa's car to pay for a cheap headstone and Dad donated his and Mom's cemetery plots for the burial. The plots had been a gift for my parents from Grandma Elliott, who, in all her "wretched excess," had never stopped to wonder—or to ask—if they would like to recline underground next to her and Grandpa Elliott for eternity. They were on sale and so that was that.

Just eight months after I had stood in front of my grand-parents' graves and pleaded for their intervention, I watched as Grandpa Betz's bottom-of-the-line casket was lowered into the earth beside them. A few dozen yards away, his ex-wife, my father's estranged mother, had been buried years before, after diabetes claimed her fingers and toes, one by one, before it took her life. Dad and I had not attended the funeral.

Four people. Two sets of parents. Innumerable secrets, small dramas, and heartbreaks. Gone as the gas fields and glass facto-ries of their youth. Gone as my idea of family. The only things left were outstanding invoices and collection notices, unpaid.

FORTY-THREE

THAT SUMMER, MY LIFE became a series of uncomfortable questions and awkward conversations. I needed to know the truth about my mother and I needed it as if it were breath or water. As I learned that the most basic, fundamental truths about us were nothing more than masterful illusions, I found myself helplessly compelled to replace those ruined beliefs with the real facts of the matter, regardless of how ugly or upsetting they might be. My mother had convinced us that the less people knew about us, the better. Now I understood why. I understood, for instance, why no one was allowed in her hospital room, or why she didn't want a funeral—those events would have meant the explosive convergence of her many lives and many lies. With her out of my way, I was determined to bring all the strands together, to braid a new identity for myself, one that was at last real and irrevocable.

I hadn't seen Harriett since we worked together at Burger King while I was in high school. She had called me once when I was in college, ostensibly to see how I was adjusting to life off campus, but then I never heard from her again. When Mom was sick, she told us not to reach out to any of her friends, including Harriett. The two had been as close as mother and daughter at one point—Mom had encouraged me to call her Grandma— but those memories were now among so many others that had been tarnished beyond recognition; had they been close? Or did I just think so?

Harriett and her husband, Gordon, live in Pennville, a tiny hamlet of about seven hundred people west of Portland, in a modular home not far from the banks of the Salamonie River, a shallow stream that meanders all over Jay County as though it's lost its way. Gordon is retired from his job as director of the welfare department and Harriett is in poor health, but sharp as a tractor blade. On days she can get out of bed, she uses a walker to get around the house, and a weeding trowel for balance when she's showing off her flower beds. When I visited their home on an overcast day in June, I enjoyed a tour of Harriett's small but vibrant garden.

She grew up in Texas, but spent much of her childhood in Touro, the famous New Orleans infirmary and birthplace of Truman Capote. Born with kneecaps too small for their joints, Harriett used a wheelchair for many years. While we spoke, her stories often circled back to the days she lived with hundreds of other sick children, dodging cruel nuns, and learning to live life as a differently abled person, as she likes to call herself. It was in the infirmary where Harriett took on weaving as a form of physical therapy. With her floor loom, she learned to coordinate her limbs and strengthened the shrunken muscles in her legs. She would go on to weave her whole life, creating rugs but also beautiful tapestries that incorporated feathers, metal, and sheepskin—tokens of the Cherokee heritage of which she was so proud.

Mom and Harriett met when Mom began volunteering for the Jay County Artists Association. At first, Harriett said she didn't know what to make of Mom, who didn't seem to have any kind of artistic focus.

"I had my weaving, so-and-so had stained glass, another had baskets, but your mom didn't have anything," Harriett remembered. "First she tried calligraphy, then cross-stitch. And then just plain sewing. She made her own clothes and she was good at it. But then she didn't want to sell any, because she didn't want anyone else having what she had."

How very like my mother, I thought.

Harriett remembered so much about my childhood—my grade school grudges and favorite cats—so I trusted her when she said my mother loved me dearly. "She just didn't know what in the hell to do with you, Axton."

Her small Chihuahua mix had climbed into my lap and fallen asleep. I rested my hand against the warmth of its back as I listened to Harriett describe her relationship with Mom.

"She showed up at my house, maybe two weeks after we met. Wanting help getting started with her calligraphy. She said she had liked it in art class in high school." Harriett began coaching my mother on what to make ("cutesie-country stuff") and how to make sales ("be prepared to take a loss"). But the mentorship quickly became something more maternal for my mother.

"She'd always say, 'Now, what I'm about to tell you is just between you and me.' On bad days, I could count on your mom calling me six to ten times," Harriett remembered. "And I began cutting her off: 'I know, Pam, it's just between us.'"

"Six to ten times a day?" Before Mom died, I don't think I made six to ten phone calls a week.

"For years and years when you were little. They became less

frequent after her dad died. And they had pretty much stopped by the time she started working at Edward Jones."

Yet it took a long time for my mother to open up to Harriett in any real way. It was five years before Harriett knew about Mom's half brothers.

"She'd say she was inviting your uncles over for holiday dinners or this or that—because she wanted them to know that she wasn't like their mom."

"Did you understand what she meant by that? 'Like their mom'?"

"Not fully. But she didn't want to be like her mom; she said it a lot."

It also took some time for my mother to begin to reveal the marital strife she was peddling to friends on Facebook. I was already away at college when Harriett said the hysterical calls from Mom began.

"She said he would scream at her and demean her in every way he could think of. That she was stupid, that she was ignorant, that she didn't know shit from apple butter." Harriett was sitting in her power recliner, wearing a housedress and ankle-high snow boots. There was a small dog on her lap as well. The local news blared from a back bedroom.

"But some of the stories she came up with were hard to believe."

"Like what?" I asked.

"Like he got so mad at her one night that he threw a heavy ladle at her. Something you would use for a big stew—a big, cafeteria spoon." Harriett used her hands to demonstrate the size.

"We didn't have anything like that," I said. "Mom never made stews, or anything at all, really."

Harriett didn't miss a beat. "This didn't fit with the John I knew. Anytime I was at the house, he was very nice. And he certainly never raised his voice at you. But when I'd really press her for details, she'd start this almost rehearsed kind of crying. It sounded the same every time." I nodded in recognition as Harriett mimicked the kind of halting, hiccupping whimper Mom would often perform when she had run out of excuses or explanations or both. "It never balanced out. I was never really sure, Axton."

"Did she tell you about other men?"

"Around the time she started the stockbroker thing. We spoke less; she was busier. But she said there were other stockbrokers who were coming down from Fort Wayne to help her, you know, make the business really good." Harriett struggled for the right words. "They were coming down late at night, parking behind the building. And there was one guy—she never told me his name—who would bring a phonograph and old-timey music. They would slow dance in the Edward Jones, just the two of them."

I couldn't help but laugh. "A *phonograph*? That sounds like a romantic comedy."

"Oh, he told her he would leave his whole past behind if she would go off with him." Harriett raised her eyebrows at me like a bemused parent listening to a child's fantasy.

"Why do you think she would make up stories like that?"

"Well." She paused for a second and looked down at the dog on her lap. It was making tiny snoring sounds. "I think she was very sad."

"Why was she so sad?"

"I don't think she got what she wanted from her mother. She said she never had a mother like her friends had, and that she wished her mother would have treated her as well as I did.

She had some type of a value system for mothers I just didn't understand."

"What about being *my* mother?"

"She wanted you to be into what she was into. She couldn't figure out how to make you like the things that she liked. In her head you were supposed to worship her, to want to be with her all the time. She had a very clear vision for what she wanted motherhood to be, and when it didn't turn out the way she thought, I think she had a hard time with that.

"And you were difficult, according to her. She said you'd bang your head and your wrists against the door frame when you didn't get your way."

"That's not true, Harriett."

"I didn't think so, either. I always looked for bruises or cuts on you; there was nothing. But Gordon and I worried about you; sometimes we worried she might be abusing you, emotionally. She refused to take you to the doctor when you started having those panic attacks. Until I told her they were going to get much worse. We were so relieved when you went off to college, Axton."

I was still an undergrad when Mom told Harriett the marriage was over. Their conversations grew more infrequent, but Harriett remembers one call from Mom, who said she was on the way home from moving me into my first apartment. "She said it took her forever to find you that place. That she wrote so many checks each month you were never going to be able to pay her back."

"But I found *and* paid for that apartment," I objected. "And she didn't pay for my college—not really, anyway."

"I'm certain she said she was giving you a lot of money for your tuition."

I gave a Harriett a *don't ask* look that she seemed to under-stand immediately.

"Anyway. That's when I called you. After she let me know you got that new apartment."

"I remember that! But then we never talked again." I looked at her quizzically.

"Oh, you don't know? Your mom called me right after that," Harriett said, slapping her thighs. "She said, 'Don't you call her, write her, or talk to her anymore! You're a bad influence!'"

"A bad influence who thought my parents were divorced and knew about Mom's after-hours dance parties," I said.

"Uh-huh." She nodded. We both fell silent then, watching the sun paint shadows on the wall and petting the small dogs asleep in our laps.

* * *

On my way home, my cell phone buzzed against my leg. It was Harriett.

"I meant to ask you—whatever happened with the ancient history professor?"

"What ancient history professor?"

"Your mom said you were involved with your ancient history professor at Purdue. That you two were going to get married."

Low, billowy clouds obscured the summer sky. "Another lie, Harriett." I laughed. "I never even took ancient history."

FORTY-FOUR

WE HAD RUN INTO MAXINE the day after Mom died, on that bitter-cold day we drove in a daze from the library to the BMV to the bank. Mom's car was well-known in Albany, a white Lincoln Town Car with a tan ragtop, so when Maxine and Garrett saw it, they pulled up and rolled a window down. So much of small-town relationships is just pure coincidence.

"How's Pam?" she yelled, the wind pushing her short gray hair against her forehead. She had on a jean jacket over a sweatshirt over a collared shirt.

"She's dead," my father said curtly.

"She's...what?" Maxine asked in disbelief.

"She's dead," Dad repeated, as he began to roll up the window to end the conversation.

I sat in the car, looking straight ahead, glad that this exchange was over. Mom had told me not to trust Maxine, that she had a big mouth exacerbated by worsening dementia. Mom's allegations seemed to be validated when I had called Maxine months earlier to tell her that Mom had cancer. Whatever good I thought I was doing was promptly dispelled when Maxine asked, "Why is your dad at the hospital—shouldn't 'her farmer' be there?" I then yelled at Maxine: "Why in the hell would he, of all people, be with Mom in the hospital? What are you talking about?" Maxine fell silent.

Looking back, I'm not sure why this didn't raise any suspicions in my mind. Maybe I was already filled to capacity with intense, unfamiliar emotions. But instead of asking Maxine what she meant, I lashed out, chiding her for asking such an inane question at a time like this. I knew the ladies at the diner had their own little world—it was like a junior high clique—but I wasn't interested in their juvenile story lines. I mentioned it to Mom and she said simply, "I told you—Alzheimer's. Don't call my friends anymore. I'll handle them." It was the beginning of our communication lockdown.

When I read the Facebook messages about "the farmer," one of my first thoughts was of Maxine. Why hadn't I listened to her? Perhaps if I had asked a few questions, I could have confronted my mom while she was still alive.

I called Maxine to apologize.

"I know about everything," I said.

"What do you know?" Maxine said cautiously.

"About all the screwing around Mom was apparently doing."

"For instance?"

"I know about 'the farmer,' the affairs Mom told people she had. I know about all of it."

"Oh, honey" was all she said.

We met at a restaurant in Albany, an old, dark bar that's also one of the town's only restaurants. Maxine enveloped me in a hug that felt warm and familiar. Her husband was there, a large and gentle man who smirks at just about every joke Maxine makes. And Maxine makes a lot of jokes. Like my mother,

Maxine is acerbic and bawdy and *very* opinionated. I had no doubt she would tell me everything I wanted to know.

She met my mother by accident (small towns again). She and Garrett had walked into the Edward Jones in Albany to collect some forms, but got to talking with my mother and her secretary, April, instead. April was very pregnant, and, because there was really no one to take over for her after she gave birth, April wondered out loud where they might keep the crib in the office. By the end of the visit, Maxine had accepted an offer to be my mother's temporary assistant.

They got along famously.

"You shouldn't hang out with your boss, but we had so much fun," Maxine said, holding her decaf coffee with both hands and smiling nostalgically. "Pam was a hoot. She could bullshit with the best of 'em."

"Speaking of bullshitting, tell me about her relationship with this 'farmer.'"

Maxine turned serious and lowered her voice. "You know, he thought your mom was divorced, just like the rest of us. That was a purely physical relationship. Pam said she bought the hotel rooms; Pam said she bought the booze. It seemed like he wasn't trying to get too involved."

"When did she tell you about the 'divorce'?" I said, using my fingers to make air quotes.

"When she was working down at the radio station. Said her boss's lawyer was able to get her a quickie divorce."

"A quickie divorce?"

"That's right. But she told me when we were at Edward Jones that they were legally separated. That's how she got away with everything she did."

"What do you mean—'everything she did'?"

"Oh, the guy up in Fort Wayne."

"The one who would come down to the office and dance with her?"

Maxine let out a hearty laugh. "As far as I know, she was going up there. Sometimes twice a week. Then she'd come back and tell me the gory story."

"Oh God. What was the gory story? Do I want to know?"

Maxine lowered her chin and her voice: "Wham, bam, thank you, ma'am. Clearing off the desk and going to it. She gave me a lot of details. *A lot.*" She sat back in her seat and looked around to see if anyone was listening.

I buried my face in my hands to hide my burning cheeks.

"And then there was Steve." Maxine seemed oblivious to my embarrassment. "You know, the guy from Indian Lake? He supposedly left me a note on my desk once when he stopped by to get your mom, but I think that was a ruse."

"What do you mean?"

"I mean I think she made it up. My God, Axton, she used to send herself flowers for attention. She said she and Steve were involved and he wanted it to be more than it was. That's what she said about your dad, too, that he had chased her way back in the day."

"Actually, she chased him. At first, anyway." I looked out across the restaurant at families lingering over a late lunch. They all seemed so normal. I felt jealous of their mundane conversations, their predictable afternoons. Mom had always insisted we were different from these people. She was right.

"Did she ever tell you anything about the identity theft?" I asked.

"She mentioned some credit card problems, but just with her own money. I didn't really understand it and I wasn't real worried about it, either—she said she had inherited a lot of money from your granddad when he died."

"Did you believe all this stuff?" I swirled the straw between shrinking ice cubes in my Coke.

"I did think she had money—how else was she going to the country club all the time? She'd say she was going to go out canvassing, drumming up business, but I think she just went to the country club. Supposedly had a guy out there, too. But there were times I'd tell her to stop puttin' on. Like the boating thing—"

"Oh, when she supposedly saved that kid's life?"

"Yeah!" Maxine pointed her coffee spoon at me. "I said, 'Come off it, Pam.'"

"And then what happened? Because you guys weren't as close at the end, right?"

"Well, for one I found out that your parents were still married! She had talked so badly about your dad, saying he didn't let her be herself, she wasn't allowed to have friends, stuff like that. She said she hated that farm, that every time she'd open the closet she'd smell her mother. But John didn't want to leave."

"Not exactly," I said. I was growing weary of explaining.

"And then they'd show up at places around town, you know, and we were all suspicious. So I decided I was gonna find out for myself. Sandy and I drove out there—your dad was in the front yard. I hollered: 'John, how long you been married?' He looked at me confused but he said, 'Thirty-nine years in June if she makes it.' And then I knew she was lying. That was it for me. I was done."

"Why didn't you tell him?"

"It just wasn't my place, honey. Just like it wasn't my place to tell you. When you called to say you knew everything, remember when I kept asking you questions to know what you meant by 'everything'? I wanted you to be able to remember your mom the way you wanted. And your dad? He's a big boy. I wasn't going to tell him his business."

"So what did you do, after you confronted my dad in the front yard?"

"I called her up! I said, 'Pam, I've talked to John. I know you're lyin'. You're sick and you're sick in the head.' I said: 'I'm done. Don't call me again.'"

"And that was it?"

"That was it."

I mulled over this new information. I wondered if it made my mother sad when Maxine abandoned her, or if she felt anything at all. In all likelihood, Mom had probably recast herself as the victim before she even heard the dial tone.

"Maxine, do you think my mom had any friends?"

"Sure do, honey," she said. "It's just that they were imaginary."

FORTY-FIVE

THE LANDSCAPE OF EAST CENTRAL INDIANA hasn't changed much since I was a kid. Far from the state's spiderweb of highways or its northern ports, these rural counties offer little temptation to developers. But in the last few decades, giant wind turbines have begun to rise above the landscape, like massive hands waving hello. They look as surreal as my grandfather's satellite dish did to my young eyes, so many years ago.

There were two turbines spinning when we arrived on Greg and Kathy's farm one warm evening in early summer. The afternoon's heat had burned off and the crops in the fields moved like synchronized swimmers with each placid breeze.

I was eager to talk with Greg and Kathy. Not only had they known my parents the longest, but they had spent lots of time with them—and me—back when they owned a skating rink in Winchester. They were my godparents, and upstanding members of the community: Greg was a state representative and Kathy a retired bank vice president. Mom and Dad had drifted away from Greg and Kathy after they sold the skating rink. No scandal, no hurt feelings, just the normal ebb and flow of adulthood.

When Dad and I visited, their daughter and Mom's former hairdresser, Kerry, joined us for dinner, and it felt like a kind of family reunion. Greg and my father can pick up like old times, and revert into a couple of giggling schoolboys around each other. We were digging into Kathy's taco salad when they began reminiscing.

"You wanna tell it?" My dad snickered.

"No, you tell it!"

Greg and my father were red-faced and writhing in their chairs.

"Out with it, Dad," I said.

"It was called Cromer Brothers, right, Greg?" He looked over at his friend.

"Right. Cromer Brothers. You could buy everything in bulk there. And we used to go out on our lunch hour—back in the those days they'd just let us roam free—and we were driving past and your dad said, 'Stop the car!' And we all wondered what he needed."

There was a second of silence before both men burst into laughter all over again. I knew where this was going.

"How many were there?" Greg asked my dad.

"A dozen cases of a dozen. A *gross* of condoms!" The men continued to howl; the women groaned.

"Condoms in bulk?" one of us said.

"I was tired of always going to the truck stop!" Dad reasoned.

My parents' high school experience could not have been further from my own.

"But I liked your mom," Greg said, reaching for decorum. "There was nothing you could say to her or around her—"

"Oh, she wouldn't balk at anything." Kathy finished his sentence. "What I remember about Pam is just how bubbly she was." I shot a glance at Dad. We knew that "bubbly" side of Mom well, but we only saw it when we were out of the house.

When Greg and Kathy bought the skating rink, my parents helped them fix it up. My mom did their books. I took skating lessons on Saturday mornings and quickly became a talented speed skater. Almost all of our weekends were spent at the rink. I asked Kathy if Mom was reporting any kind unhappiness or marital discord back then.

"Oh, no. She never said they were having problems. Things were great. They had plenty of money; she loved the farm and the animals."

"No, she did not love the farm or the animals," my dad chimed in.

"But she did! She said she trained those donkeys herself!" Kathy argued.

"What was it called again?" Kerry asked.

"Up to Our Assess Donkey and Mule Farm!" Dad replied to a round of laughter.

"Oh, she loved writing tuition checks to that Christian school with those checks—the ones with the farm name on them. She just thought it was hilarious," Kerry said.

"So *that's* why they didn't like me."

"And there was one time you refused to do something there…"

"The revival?"

"Yeah, and you wouldn't do it and she was so proud of you. She thought it was great."

I couldn't help but smile. These were things I wish I had known at the time.

Kerry must have noticed my smile. "Your mom was a very kind person. Do you remember how she knitted an afghan anytime anyone had a baby? When she made them for my kids—those were treasured gifts."

I didn't know what to say. It had been months since I thought of my mother's capacity for magnanimity. That was a side of herself that she always saved for others: her clients at the country club, the ladies at the diner. Dad and I were so seldom on the receiving end of compliments or gifts that it was hard to square what I was hearing with my memories of her.

"Did you ever think my parents were divorced?" I launched the question into the conversation like a grenade. I didn't feel like dwelling on my mom's softer side.

"Well, you were separated for a while, right?" Kerry asked my father.

"No, never."

"But Pam said, time after time. You were messing around."

"She was the one messing around!"

"But it was you, John, you!" Kathy protested, as if her version of the truth, of her close friend, could somehow be argued into existence. By now everyone's forks were resting on their plates.

"I remember when my mom told me you and Pam were splitting up," Kerry said. "I just couldn't believe it. I thought you guys would be together forever."

"When did she tell you about this?" I asked Kathy.

"Well, we sold the skating rink in 1993 . . . so sometime after that. She called. We had drifted apart; you know how life goes." She made a figure eight with her hand to represent the currents of time. "And then I didn't see her again until right before she died. I saw her at a gas station. I almost didn't recognize her."

"She was very sick," Dad said.

"I could tell. She had on *stretch pants*." Kathy gave me a knowing look.

"Very sick," I reiterated.

"I would see John and Pam together from time to time," Kerry interjected. "But I never said anything. Just thought they had got back together."

"Your mom always said that your grandfather had *a lot* of money. A lot. She always let me know how wealthy her family was," Kathy told me. "So I wasn't too worried about her when she said they split up."

"That's not exactly true," I said.

"She had access to all of our books when we owned the rink. She knew everything. I don't know why we were spared."

"Because you didn't live with her; she couldn't control you like she did us."

"I still can't believe it, Axton. My kids can't believe it." Kathy shook her head.

Between us sat the remains of a strawberry pie and five licked-clean forks. I looked at my father, who, sitting next to his childhood friend, seemed more relaxed and happy than I had seen him in a while. I felt nothing but a persistent, numb confusion.

Outside in the flickering twilight, the windmills churned around an ominous red light. In the daylight, these turbines look like looming giants; in the dark, they look like monsters.

FORTY-SIX

I HADN'T EXPECTED TO SPEAK with Tiffany again after the memorial.

Tiffany was the president of the Ball State chapter of Feminists for Action, an activist group for women's reproductive rights that my mother was a part of. Toward the end of her life, Mom became an outspoken proponent of abortion rights and gender equality. Her Facebook wall was crowded with memes espousing feminism and deriding conservative politicians.

It was only days after Mom died that Tiffany had sent a Facebook message to me to let Dad and me know that the group was hosting an event to commemorate their friend and to see if we could attend. These were the tender days between my mother's death and our discovery of the truth; we were still eager to remember and celebrate her in whatever small way we could. I drove the three hours from Illinois to Muncie just for the afternoon; Dad invited coworkers from the store and even his barber. Because Mom had been so unyielding about not wanting a funeral, this makeshift memorial became a kind of stand-in.

I met my dad in a dim Ball State parking garage and we

walked together to the classroom building where the impromptu event was being held. Feminists for Action was largely composed of undergrads, and a dozen or so of them were standing in the back of the room, sipping punch, when we arrived. Tiffany came over to introduce herself and to thank us for being there.

"You must be Axton," she said with a sympathetic smile.

"I am. And this is my dad, John," I said as I gestured toward Dad.

Tiffany paused abruptly. Her eyes narrowed very slightly. "It's nice to meet you, John," she said in a forced way. She turned back to me quickly. "I have this for you."

Tiffany removed a folder from the fold of her elbow. As I flipped through it, she said, "Just about all of us wrote one."

They were letters about my mother. They were downright adulatory.

We had left the memorial feeling somber but buoyant with pride. Months later, I understood why Tiffany had looked at my father like he was some kind of imposter. When I wrote to her, she replied immediately.

> *When I planned her memorial, when I met you and your father, I should have brought it up that it was confusing. I was under the impression they were divorced, had been for a while, and thought she had a boyfriend. I had so many questions but that wasn't the time to ask them, you were both grieving and I started to doubt my own memory.*

I told her that Mom had a habit of making people doubt their own memories. I asked her to tell me about the Pam that the group knew.

It was Valentine's Day, and I remember Pam saying she was leaving to have a lunch date with "her farmer." She told me that they were going to eat at this diner place near where he lived, that it was a small town and the people there gave her looks because they seemingly didn't approve of her dating him. She told me that this farmer's daughters didn't like her and thought she was after his money, which she just laughed at.

There was no way to explain to this young woman the deep, almost ironic contradictions my mother was feeding her. That the only thing my mother cared about more than what people thought of her was money. When I filled Tiffany in on a just a fraction of the deceit I had discovered, she was astounded.

She was a great friend, an awesome feminist/advocate. She helped many people. But the more I think on it, the more it does seem that her presentation of self, to me, was almost contradictory to her actual self and I can't help but feel hurt.

Even in a Facebook message I could sense her very real disappointment. I had transformed my mother from a much-loved friend into a malevolent stranger with just a few lines. There was no comfort I could offer Tiffany other than I knew how she felt. Every once in a while, I look through the letters the girls wrote to and about my mother, floored by just how well she had them all fooled.

. . . You took the time to listen, to give me advice. I can't help but marvel at the impact your words had and still have.

. . . I thank my lucky stars I was fortunate enough to know you.

. . . You showed us all what amazing women we could aspire to be.

. . . We have your words, your examples, your memories to guide us through the remainder of our journeys.

. . . You were our group mother, Pam. Constantly encouraging us with your wisdom and love.

. . . You deserved to know how much it touched me when you called me your "science daughter."

. . . You offered sisterhood and guidance when we faced challenges; you provided a kind of motherly support to so many people.

Motherly support to so many people, but why not me?

FORTY-SEVEN

BILL WAS AN ACQUAINTANCE of Mom's from her days at Edward Jones. I found his message among the others in my mom's Facebook inbox, inquiring about her use of her maiden name. Had he missed something, he asked?

No, just easier for my high school friends to find me, she explained. I'm not sure what about her relationship with Bill made her tell the truth, that she was still married to my father, but she seemed to play it up: *If it was John with cancer, I'd be beside myself.*

I reached out to Bill to see if he might help me track down a missing $32,000. I was able to glean from some paperwork in the outbuilding that Mom had cashed out an IRA in 2008, after she was let go from the radio station. It wasn't a rollover—Mom had walked out of an Edward Jones branch with a check—but I thought maybe she had put it into another account before the tax penalty kicked in.

Bill was surprised and sad to hear that my mother had died, and couldn't remember her ever saying anything about being separated from my dad. Like me, he couldn't figure out where the money had gone. He did recall another brokerage account she kept, but it had been so long he didn't remember where that was now.

"There's something else," he said, as the conversation was dwindling to a close.

"What's that?"

"I remember your mom saying this thing. And I'm sorry if I shouldn't tell you this. But she said that she had money hidden in Ohio and that you and your dad would never find it. I didn't know what to make of it at the time, and I honestly couldn't tell you the context, it's been so long."

"But you're sure she said Ohio?"

"She said Ohio."

I thanked Bill, and hung up the phone. Maybe the $32,000 was hidden in Ohio, along with the tuition money I never got. But where? Did she buy property, start up a shell business? I spun my cell phone around nervously in my hand, imagining all the additional ways my mother could have conned us.

FORTY-EIGHT

SOMEHOW A YEAR WENT BY. I came home less often. Dad had Candice now, so I didn't have to worry about him wandering around the farm, like Heathcliff on the moors. Between classes and my own research, I pressed forward in my attempt to unearth all my mother's secrets. I kept in contact with her friends, in case anything interesting came up at the diner or the country club. I ran background checks and credit checks and followed up on intriguing line items I set aside while we emptied the house, outbuilding, and mailboxes.

I also contacted all the writers and reporters who had previously covered our story, which at the time had been unresolved. The resolution of a cold case as old as ours got attention; the fact that Mom was the perpetrator made it a headline. The media interviews were becoming many and more significant. My truth-finding mission had spectators, which only motivated me more.

The following summer after Mom died, I returned to Jay County to attend her fortieth high school reunion in Ohio. The back roads were straight like runways and lined by cornfields.

They stretched taffy-thin into the horizon. "I am Pam Elliott's daughter," I said out loud to my steering wheel for the tenth time in as many minutes. "I am Pam Elliott's daughter."

From Mom's Facebook messages, I gathered that friends from her childhood thought she was single and had a second home in Ohio. Mom had talked to them about a condo at Indian Lake, a pickup truck, too. When I saw that she belonged to a group devoted to Indian Lake happenings, I scoured Facebook until I found the date and time for her fortieth. I messaged the organizers and explained who I was, that Indian Lake was a big part of my mother's life, and that I wanted to attend the reunion to learn more about her and it. I received a confused email in response but sent in my twenty-five-dollar registration fee anyway. In reality, my hope was that someone there might reveal something—some clue or small detail—about my mother that could finally help me understand what she had done.

Indian Lake High School was a collection of unremarkable brick buildings at the intersection of two state routes. I parked out in front of the gym. "I am Pam Elliott's daughter," I stated one last time, with conviction, before I got out of the car. I unzipped my purse and felt for the old photos of Mom and me, the ones I'd brought for proof. The summer sun was still high overhead as I walked across the lot, the parking lines and fire lanes freshly painted.

"Oh! You're the daughter of the woman who died," the lady working the door said, when I told her my name. She handed me a name tag. *Daughter of Pam Elliott*, it announced.

The gym looked like any other gym. The bleachers had been folded into the walls and the smell of rubber mats and sweat hung in the air. Tea lights illuminated a smattering of long and round tables. The reunion wasn't for one particular class, but for many of them—1964, 1974, 1979, 1984, and 1989, among others. I found my way to the 1974 table, where only a few of Mom's old classmates were gathered.

"Hello," I said to the bunch, with a palm raised in greeting. "I'm Pam Elliott's daughter."

A half-dozen eyes looked back at me with confusion.

"Are you sure?" asked one of the men. "You don't look a thing like her."

I was prepared. I handed him the photos of Mom and me. In one, she sat happily on a dock at Indian Lake.

"I didn't know she had a daughter!" the man said, flipping through the photos. He held them up to glance back and forth from them to my face.

"We didn't even know Pam got married!" someone else said. They had seen her at the last reunion, ten years ago, and she hadn't mentioned it. At the time of her fortieth reunion I was thirty-two. She hadn't revealed it in their Facebook group, either. No one that I talked to had any idea that my mother was married, or that I existed. The only reason they believed me that night was because I had hard-copy proof.

Mom was married less than two weeks after graduating high school. How could any eighteen-year-old keep her mouth shut about such a momentous event?

"Well, I remember her hanging around with two different boys that year," said Sonny, an older friend of Mom's who'd known her in high school. I had called him before the reunion to get an idea of what I might expect to hear from Mom's classmates, and without hesitation he'd told me about a man named Steve. "Steve is a yacht salesman or consultant in Florida these days, but they were close in high school."

Maxine had mentioned Steve. But I couldn't seem to get in

touch with him. I did discover a throng of photos online of Mom and Steve together—at their thirtieth reunion. Dad and I had no idea she had even attended the event, but we both recalled her going on an "overnight business trip" around that time. She and Steve kept in touch over the years and I had found some innocent exchanges between them when I looked through Mom's email. I could tell by their photos and correspondence— as well as what Mom was telling her friends about it—that Mom had a bit of an obsession with the guy, and with that time in her life. Back on Indian Lake, when she was young and free.

"At first she was real quiet but that all changed from hanging around and participating with us," a mutual friend of Mom's and Steve's told me about Mom in high school. "She limbered right up when she got comfortable around us. Back then we could pervert anyone." This "perversion" seemed to linger on into their adult years. Mom's messages to her old high school friends started with salutations like "Kiss!" and "Hey sweetie!" She was open with them about who she was sleeping with, living with, supposedly engaged to. But the only one who wouldn't speak to me about Mom's last years was Steve.

He bore an uncanny resemblance to my dad, but, unlike my father, he seemed to live a life of suntanned luxury. At least that's what his Facebook profile seemed to indicate. In the year following my mom's death, I had tried in earnest to get ahold of Steve, but he never returned my calls. I wanted to ask him if he and my mother had been dating when she ran off and got married right after graduation, if he had known about my father, if he had perhaps later conversed with or counseled my mom about money.

Steve didn't turn up at the reunion. And none of my conversations yielded any revelations. Near the end of the night

I walked to the back of the gym where a handwritten, trifold poster board read *In Memoriam*. Underneath the poster was a binder, full of the names of alumni who had passed away. I flipped to 1974 and found Mom, listed, of course, as "Pam Elliott." I snapped a photo with my phone and texted it to Dad. *Wow*, he texted back.

When my grandmother got sick, my grandfather had promptly sold their mobile home and never returned to Indian Lake. When I told my dad I was planning to attend the reunion, he was worried. He said it might not be safe for me to go but admittedly had little reason to think that. What was it about this place that terrified the men in my family? What was it that drew the women there?

I knew Dad would stay up and wait for me to get home, so I stuffed the photos back in my purse and made my way toward the exit.

The sun was in my eyes, low on the horizon, as I drove west back to Indiana. The evening's refrain still rang in my head: I was Pam Elliott's daughter.

But who was Pam Elliott? I was still no closer to finding out.

FORTY-NINE

I FOUND STEVE IN FORT LAUDERDALE. The internet told
me he worked at a boat dealership just south of the airport,
sandwiched between ten tangled lanes of I-95 and the Atlantic
Ocean. I didn't go to Florida just to confront him, but attending
a work conference in Clearwater Beach was a convenient excuse
to finally figure out just what, if anything, this guy knew about
my mother and her money.

It took me about four hours to get from my hotel in
Clearwater to the dealership where I might find Steve. I hadn't
called ahead to find out if he would be working or not, in case
he'd use the heads-up to avoid me. A violent line of storms
slowed me down as I bisected the state on the road known as
Alligator Alley. Through breaks in the rain I'd see signs luring
tourists for airboat rides and gator nuggets. Again, I rehearsed
what I would say when I got there, what I would ask. Had there
been something between them? How did she get those pictures
of his house that I had found on her computer?

In hundreds of deeply buried Facebook messages to her friend
Sandy, my mother had concocted some seriously bizarre story

lines in which Steve was the star. At a certain point, she said, she had accepted a proposal—and a ring, of course—from Steve, but had had a change of heart. During their engagement, when Mom was supposedly preparing to move back to Indian Lake to be with Steve, she said she met and fell for her farmer friend. Ultimately, she told her unwitting friend, she had chosen him. In one message she describes how difficult it was to hurt Steve when she returned his ring. In another, she can't contain her excitement about redecorating "the farmer's" house. The most remarkable thing about these messages is how long and detailed they are, interspersed with vivid descriptions and dialogue. My mother was smart, was a good writer, but it must have taken her some time to think this stuff up.

When, I wondered, did she come up with the plot twist that Steve would die suddenly not long after she broke off their engagement, and that he would leave his house and truck to her? Had she rehearsed the shock of his death, the deep sadness she said she felt? I do know that she had taken the time to save the photos of Steve's house—or someone's house—on her computer, so that when her friends asked, she could show off her inheritance.

It was a small dealership, made mostly of massive glass panels. There was a parking area squeezed between a collection of Jet Skis and pontoon boats. I took a deep breath before I opened the front door, assuring myself that this was no odder than anything else I had done since Mom died.

"Is Steve working today?" I asked the woman at the front desk.

"He is! Let me call him down," she said enthusiastically, then paged him over the loudspeaker. A few minutes later, the man I recognized from Facebook was descending the stairs into the lobby. He smiled a confused smile, trying to place me. He had friendly eyes beneath bushy eyebrows and a swoop of sunny-gray hair. This was not what I had been expecting. At some point during my digging, I had decided that Steve was my mother's accomplice, or at least her confidant. Mom had painted him as a yacht salesman, wealthy and well connected. When I imagined this moment, Steve had slicked-back hair and sunglasses on; the theme song to *Miami Vice* was playing. Instead, the man walking toward me looked kind and warm, like someone's favorite uncle.

"Hi, I'm Pam Elliott's daughter," I said with my hand extended. Steve's confused face melted into wonder.

"Oh my God," he said, holding my hand a beat too long, "you really are—Pam Elliott's daughter?"

I followed Steve into an empty office with a corner window where we took our places on opposite sides of a large desk, as if we were about to sign some paperwork on a boat. There were only a few people milling around the place; it was still early on a Monday morning.

"Your mom disappeared after high school—just vanished. Then she showed up at the thirtieth like nothing had happened."

"Did she tell you she was married?"

"She said she was divorced, and in the process of getting her old last name back. But no kids. She never said anything about having a daughter."

"Is that why you never returned my calls? Because you didn't think I could be who I said I was?"

"Honestly, I really didn't think she had kids. The whole thing seemed so odd; I just didn't want to get involved."

And here I was, involving him.

"Did she ever mention being engaged when you were in school together? My parents married right after graduation."

"Never mentioned it."

"What was she like when you saw her at the last reunion?"

"She was..." Steve shifted in his seat and made the kind of gestures I was used to when one of Mom's friends was about to say something bad about her.

"Go ahead," I urged.

"It was like she was coming to show off or something. You know, she wanted to talk about this job she had at that radio station and the celebrities she was meeting. It was weird. Way over-the-top and it was like she couldn't see how uncomfortable she was making people feel. She was coming across as someone who thought they were better than everyone else in Russells Point—speaking of, do you still have the trailer?"

"What trailer? The one in Indiana?" I asked, thinking he meant the one I grew up in.

"No, on the lake. The one—it would be the one your grand-parents had. Pam said she inherited it from them; I just assumed you inherited it from her."

So Mom was lying to Steve, too. "Grandpa and Grandma sold the trailer sometime around 1975 when Grandma got cancer."

"Huh. But your mom said she stayed there the night of our reunion?"

"She said a lot of things."

"It was just strange to see her at the reunion. Like she had this life nobody knew about."

I laughed. "You should Google me."

"What?" Steve's eyebrows folded into a V at the bridge of his nose.

"Just Google: 'Axton Betz-Hamilton,'" I said, realizing how strange this must be for him. I watched Steve's face as he spelled out my name on his keyboard. He used his index finger to strike the Enter key and then sat back in his chair as the results populated almost instantly. I was silent as he scrolled through them, muttering soft exclamations.

He looked back at me. "Wow. This is unreal."

"Can you tell me if these are pictures of your house?" I set my phone on the desk. Steve picked it up and began to scroll through them.

"This definitely isn't my house, but it looks like a house at the lake—I recognize that scenery. Looks like mid-March? Early spring? Maybe around the boat show?"

"What boat show?"

"Every March there's a big boat show in Indian Lake. Everyone's been all cooped up all winter and ready to buy, buy, buy."

"I think Mom has photos on her computer of the boat show," I thought aloud.

"This house"—he pointed at my phone—"this looks like a rental. Maybe she came for the boat show and stayed in this house?"

"Maybe," I said as I reclaimed my phone. Our conversation went on much longer than I expected. Steve was far from the scheming huckster I had been imagining. Within the first twenty minutes, it was evident that Steve was not in cahoots with my mother; in fact, he hardly even knew her.

"She was the new kid. She was having a hard time because it was senior year and the social groups had long been established. I wouldn't have really been paying attention but one of my teachers said it was my job as class president to make the new girl feel welcome."

"So you were just doing as you were told?"

"Yeah. I mean, I did feel sorry for her. And she liked us a lot—she started tagging along with us."

The phrase "tagging along" couldn't have been more different from how Mom described her relationship with those high school friends. These were the people she had spent a lifetime yearning to be near, wishing she could be. During our day-trip to Indian Lake and so often during my childhood, she would tell me about them, her wistful stories usually culminating in laughter and an almost tangible longing.

I had heard so much about them. And they hadn't heard one word about me.

I never asked Steve about the money. I knew what he would say. He was just another unassuming character in one of my mother's invented dramas, and, just like the rest of us, he had no idea where it was.

* * *

I have circled back through my mother's friends again and again. I've exhausted the roster of witnesses. My list of suspected co-conspirators is all crossed out. The neighbors, Nila, Harold, Lisa, Bobby and Mary, even the felonious Greg Reinhold: Mom had manipulated us at one time or another into thinking they were likely identity thieves when she knew very well that they weren't. While I've learned a lot about the many different versions of my mom, I still don't know her, who she really was when she wasn't pretending, acting, lying, or stealing. Who she saw when she looked in the mirror. At one point, I thought about having a conversation with "the farmer" about Mom, but decided against it when Maxine told me Mom was the one who manipulated him and that he had believed she was divorced. He was a victim of Mom's manipulation, just like the rest of us.

My mother pushed most of her good friends out of her life as soon as they questioned her lies. Sandy, the woman who played willing audience to Mom's sagas about Steve and "the farmer," told me once that she knew all along that it was a ruse.

"On Facebook, she would say she was at 'the farmer's' house in Albany, but I could see the message was sent from Redkey. She'd come in the restaurant and would wear different diamond rings and bracelets that she said he bought for her, but I knew he didn't."

Sandy said she didn't appreciate the lies but she let Mom "ramble on." Just like her high school classmates let her tag along with them. Just like her friends who never asked why she and her ex-husband were together at the store. Just like Dad let her drive away with a trunk full of sex toys. Just like I let her cosign for my car when I lived in Havana even though I felt something was off. None of us knew my mother, but I guess none of us were really allowed to know her.

FIFTY

"YOU'RE HURT. DEEPLY. You feel betrayed."

What this man was telling me wasn't wrong; I just didn't know why he wanted to focus on it. I felt uncomfortable.

"You need closure. She *is* sorry. She's telling me she's sorry."

I hadn't visited a psychic, nor entertained the idea, but Mike had been virtually hand-delivered to us, saying he could communicate with spirits. When my dad met him in the bulk candy aisle of the grocery store—introduced by a mutual friend—Mike had blurted out: "You have a bright female light over you."

My father stopped him. "Well, I'm not sure who that would be," he said sardonically. It was, in fact, the opposite of what he had heard the last time he saw a medium, decades ago. He had gone with some coworkers on their lunch hour, just as a gag, something to do to say they'd done it. That psychic had sensed a black light—someone actively trying to harm him. Dad figured it (if "it" was even real) was his abusive mother, but in hindsight, perhaps the black light was Mom.

Standing there in front of large containers of jelly beans, Mike offered to do a reading for Dad and me. "Don't tell me

anything about your wife. I don't want it to interfere with what
I pick up."

Now we were sitting in Mike's small living room, nestled in
a nondescript complex of affordable housing on the east side of
Muncie. Mike was battling ALS, which made him appear older
than he probably was. Without much hair or muscle tone, he
almost disappeared into his recliner.

As an academic, I found the whole thing ridiculous. I didn't
believe in it. But what would it hurt, I figured. And maybe
Mike would be able to give my dad some kind of peace. It's
likely Dad would have thought Mike was a total wacko, except
he knew that the police had, a few years back, consulted
him during a very public search for a missing college student.
Connie, my dad's coworker who introduced them, swore Mike
was the real deal. Ever the skeptic, even I couldn't deny it: he
did seem to know some things that he shouldn't. Even if he had
researched our case, the details he knew about my mother were
not available online. But when he claimed to know Mom was
sorry for "some of what she did" (she apparently didn't specify
which parts), I didn't particularly care. If I was going to learn
anything today, it was going to be logistical—what she did with
the money and how she did it—not emotional. My mother
could hang out, eternally sorry in the netherworld for as long
as she wanted.

"Is there more to find, Mike?"

"Oh, yes." Mike spoke with a lazy, lilting cadence, stretching
out his vowels like lullabies. "Did you have a good relationship
with your mom?"

The question seemed impossible to answer. Ever since
I learned about my mom's crimes, whatever relationship I
thought I had with her now seemed almost comically inverted.

Good memories immediately segued into speculation about her motives. When I reflected on our special trips to the mall, for instance, I now wondered if all that mother-daughter time was a ploy, to keep me under her thumb and off her tail. Any nostalgia I felt about my mother instantly hardened into a scientific analysis. I could no longer answer personal questions about her or us with any kind of accuracy. I had become an unreliable narrator about my own life.

"Yes and no. Really, I just want to know the truth," I said quickly, hoping he would get my point.

"But *why* do you need to know the truth?" He did not get my point.

"Because. The truth is important." I looked down at the creature on my lap, Mike's long-haired black cat. Like me, he adored them; his whole house was filled with cat-lover paraphernalia. He never accepted payment for these kinds of sessions, he said; he just asked that people make a donation to a local animal welfare league.

"I do get 'childhood' for some reason," he said, giving up needling me for the moment. "I don't know if that means some kind of abuse?"

Dad and I looked at each other with raised eyebrows.

"She's telling me 'childhood,' so you may want to look there first. See if you can find her childhood medical records. Talk to a psychiatrist about her multiple personality disorder."

"Multiple personalities?" It was a theory I had entertained but never verbalized.

"Yes, go talk to some doctors, get more information about what was wrong with her brain."

I thought about the piles of medical records I had packed away somewhere.

"And you." Mike was looking at my father now. "You can close this chapter. She wants you to move on."

"So I'm off the hook?" my dad joked.

"She's sorry. She tried to open up before she died; she tried to say something, but she couldn't."

I didn't have to look at my dad to know we were both thinking about her last strained seconds in the hospital.

"Axton, there's so much in you, it's hard to interpret. But I feel like you're going to need, and going to get, more education soon. You have things to learn."

"More? She has a PhD. She's already a professor." My father was dubious.

"You have more to learn." Mike was insistent. "You're going to move into another part of your career. Be ready. Do it. It'll be a good thing."

I nodded at this directive. Education and professional development, I could handle. It was the feelings and the apologies that made me squirm.

"She's all around you."

Of course she was all around me. Since she died, the majority of my conversations and thoughts had been about her. I didn't need a psychic to tell me my mother was near. I conjured her endlessly.

FIFTY-ONE

MORE THAN TWO DECADES AGO, the term "multiple personality disorder" fell out of favor for its connotation of separate and distinct identities existing in one person. Today, doctors call it dissociative identity disorder to better communicate how someone who suffers from the disease experiences the splintering of a single identity. Some patients report that this fragmentation, when it occurs, feels like a possession; others indicate there are long, transitional phases as they move from one version of themselves to another.

People with DID typically have a dominant, primary identity who is dependent, depressed, and guilt-ridden. The alternate iterations of their identity—often called the alters—take on a completely different history, memory, and personality than the primary. The Pam Betz we knew was often couch-bound, prone to long spells of sadness and angst. The Pam Elliott her friends knew was spunky, generous, full of youthful energy. She had a starkly different backstory (her childless marriage, her abusive husband, her divorce and new boyfriend) than my mother.

DID is also marked by inexplicable memory loss. Sufferers

can recall few memories and instead experience the past in notes of overwhelming emotion, much like my mother's bizarre attachment to the high school friends who hardly knew her, or her obsession with her parents' absence.

Like many emotional disturbances, this one generally develops during childhood, and is triggered by severe trauma—often abuse. As with PTSD, DID occurs when a person cannot integrate the various aspects of their identity—consciousness, memory, experience—into one self, often because some factors are just too painful to reconcile. Instead, the person develops these alters as a way to absorb or cope with elements of their lives outside of their control, such as physical or sexual abuse.

I have no evidence that my mother was abused as a child. What I do have are anecdotes about my grandmother's icy nature, her compulsions and indiscretions. I know that she spent her husband's money with a recklessness that bordered on spite and nearly drove him to bankruptcy. I know that my mom's brother, my uncle Mike, would not speak about his childhood. I know that my mother became sexually active at twelve and was promiscuous her whole life, a common adult trait of childhood sexual abuse. I know that my mother *begged* to leave Portland for Indian Lake during high school—was she trying to escape something or someone? Was the Pam Elliott she morphed into once there the onset of her alter? I know that my mother loathed the limestone house she grew up in—the same one I grew up in. Dad remembers that her moods were stable (and mostly positive) before they moved back. He says that after they sold the house, she seemed like a woman unburdened; I had noticed the change, too. Did something happen to her there? Was her childhood home—like mine—a place of terror and isolation?

It's likely I will never find out if my mother was abused. And without her here, a diagnosis of DID is impossible. If she did suffer from the disease, her identity likely forked into the two women I now know her to be. When an alter takes control of the primary, the disruption typically involves a drastic shift in one's sense of self, sense of agency, and behavior. In studies conducted on those living with DID, more than one-third reported engaging in criminal activity when under the influence of their alter. Was my mother's deceit her own conscious decision? Could she be held accountable if her actions were outside of her control?

It's worth noting that DID is an extremely rare condition, and many mental health professionals believe that false diagnoses have been proliferated by the sensational representations of it in popular culture (movies like *Sybil* and the *The Three Faces of Eve* in particular inspired a frenzy of DID diagnoses after their release). In reality, fewer than 1 percent of the population likely suffers from DID. Some researchers even believe the symptoms of the disease are actually learned social behavior, perfected by highly manipulative people.

If I'm playing armchair psychiatrist, I'm far more willing to diagnose my mother with psychopathy more than anything else. She exhibits all the classic symptoms: lack of remorse, reckless-ness, irresponsibility, and the uncanny ability to lie. My mother was overconfident to the point of narcissism, compulsive, impul-sive, and selfish. She was—and I am sure of this—incapable of love.

In going through all of her available medical records for any evidence of mental illness, only one grim notation stood out. There, amid her cancer symptoms—the lumps in her arms, the pain in her jaw—a physician had written: *Symptoms are aggravated by conflict or stress at home or work. Persistent negatives include thoughts of death or suicide.*

Unlike normal parents, psychopaths do not encourage independence or self-confidence in their children. Instead, they work to undermine the child's self-esteem, making derogatory comments about their skills or appearance. Any encouragement that a psychopath might offer is for their own ends and they will be the first to take credit for their child's achievement.

The last photo I have of my mother before she was diagnosed with cancer is the one I brought to her hospital room in Indianapolis in which she and my father are standing at my side as I proudly hold up an award for my research in childhood identity theft—work that was born from the decades of paranoia, fear, and financial ruin that she caused. In it, my mother is so happy that she appears to be laughing.

FIFTY-TWO

ALL TOLD, MY MOTHER made over half a million dollars disappear. When she died, our family was on the hook for about $10,000 in credit card debt (that we know of) among the three of us. Dad was left with $100,000 in student loans that Mom took out to pay for her master's degree and doctoral classes, even though she had convinced him it was necessary for him to borrow $50,000 from his 401(k) to pay for graduate school—which he did. Then there was the nearly $50,000 that never made it to Purdue.

During the height of the farm's success, my dad estimates that he gave Mom at least $200,000 dollars from the sale of hay and donkeys. He thought that money was going into their savings and retirement accounts; there were no such accounts. On that terrible day that we received the foreclosure notice, the day my parents' discord hit a fever pitch, Dad agreed to withdraw $40,000 from his 401(k) to cover what they owed to the mortgage company.

Mom cashed out $32,000 from the retirement account at the radio station after they let her go. I have the paperwork detailing the withdrawal but the trail goes cold from there. When I was a baby, my grandfather set up a Gerber life insurance policy for me, which he said he put in my mother's name before he died. Not surprisingly, the money had vanished by the time I thought to check on it.

It's impossible to determine the interest my father's imaginary retirement accounts would have accrued, but it's likely he wouldn't still be working now if Mom had been saving money like she said she was.

We don't know where this money went. We do know she spent freely in the years after my grandfather died—jewelry and shoes and lunches out at the Albany Golf Club. Of course that explains where some of the missing cash ended up. But in rural Indiana, a person would have to devote an exceptional amount of effort to spend half a million dollars in their lifetime and still have so little to show for it.

Like all of my projects that explore any aspect of identity theft, this book has been an undertaking that is largely for the benefit of others—my aim is to help anyone who has dealt with this debilitating crime. But in a small way, it has also been written with the hope that someone, somewhere, may read it and realize that they have answers to my questions. I would like to know the truth because the truth is important.

FIFTY-THREE

RECENTLY, ONE OF MY FATHER'S barn cats gave birth to a litter of three kittens. We found them out there, wedged beneath their mother's heaving ribs, eyes sealed shut and mewing with a heartbreaking sweetness. Their fur was still wet in places, and it shone in the morning light that seeped through the windows in the donkey stalls. Each one of them was a glistening, snowy silver.

When a mother cat experiences stress or sickness while she is pregnant, something in the kittens' development goes a little haywire. They won't necessarily get sick, but things that are supposed to happen during gestation—like pigment deposits in the fur—sometimes don't. Kittens delivered by a mother in distress often have a thick layer of dazzling gray fur. It's called a fever coat.

As the kittens get older and grow stronger, as they wean and learn to rely less on their mother, the fever coat will begin to fall out in clumps. Soon, they become the color they were always supposed to be—startlingly black or fiery orange. The internet abounds with stories of "magic, color-changing kittens," but really these kittens are just growing into their real selves, the animals they would have been before trauma entered their young lives.

My father and I stood in wonder before these babies, cooing and gasping each time one did a backflip or pushed its way to its mother's milk. Dad has rescued countless animals (recently he adopted two turkeys because their owner had plans to eat them), but each time one arrives or one is born, he is filled with a childlike excitement. When people come to the farm for the first time, he delights in introducing them to each animal, especially his mammoth donkeys. There's Lightning, a milky creature who was beaten with a shovel as a stud, and came to my father full of rage and fear. Thunder, with his dark eyes and velvet nose, who was so badly abused and terrified of people he would drip with sweat whenever anyone came near. These gentle souls are— and always have been—my father's retreat, a constant source of joy unadulterated by money troubles, a crumbling marriage, extraordinary betrayal.

I don't have that kind of respite. The life I have built for myself as a fraud and identity theft expert requires that I wade, over and over, into the cruelest parts of humanity, endlessly examining why and how we trick and cheat one another, what new versions of deception we've invented now. My reprieve comes in knowing that my work may help someone. Someone like me, sitting alone on a couch with their credit report in hand, someone begging for an auto loan, someone who has been hurt deeply.

It is a great irony that in choosing this line of work, I have surrendered yet another piece of my identity to the crimes committed against me. By making my mother's betrayal the center of my life, in many ways, I have drawn out her ugly legacy. Instead of shedding my fever coat, I have clung to it, held on to that glossy silver fur, putting my own trauma under a microscope again and again and again.

Sometimes when I think about what I have lost, I rage against the unfairness of it all. In many ways the financial impact of my family's identity theft was the least of the damage. You can rebuild your credit; you cannot rebuild your childhood. I cannot, for instance, meet up with my childhood best friend, to catch up over a coffee or a cocktail, and talk about the boys we liked in high school or the regrettable outfits we wore. That best friend doesn't exist. I wasn't allowed to have her, wasn't able to spend hours a night on the phone with her when I should have been doing my homework.

In fact, it's hard for me to go home at all. The space between the Jay County line and my father's front porch inspires a special and violent kind of anxiety inside me. Even on the sunniest day, an ominous cloud seems to follow me across the barren landscape.

My marriage is still long-distance. Three years ago I accepted a job in South Dakota while Rob stayed in Iowa. I am beyond grateful for a partner who understands my need to devote so much of my time and energy to my work, who remains steadfast and loyal, despite our nontraditional arrangement. Our relationship thrives because we are both equal parts loyal and loners— but also because I do best with a little distance, a safety buffer of sorts, between myself and the world. It's something I need less and less, but I need it all the same.

Rob and me at a Quad Cities AAA baseball game.

When we are together, I'll often surprise Rob with an un-provoked admission. "I spent two dollars on a clearance T-shirt today," I'll announce, just so that he knows exactly, down to the last penny, where our money goes. I also like to present him with the day's stack of mail—the circulars and fliers and scammy subprime loan offers all accounted for—to satisfy, I'm sure, some unhealed urge from my childhood.

Though we relish time with our many nieces and nephews and my cousin's children, it's unlikely that Rob and I will have children of our own. My mother used to tell me I was "too good to have children," praising and disparaging me at the same time, as she was wont to do. She wouldn't let family or friends gift me baby dolls when I was young, saying she wanted me to know there was more a woman could accomplish than bearing children. Perhaps she was trying to empower me, or maybe it was simply another repudiation of her own identity.

Other words of my mother's continue to haunt my self-esteem, my eating habits. While I long ago ditched the diet pills and starvation routines, I still despise having a meal in front of other people, enduring their judgment like I used to my mother's. Despite multiple degrees, awards, a happy marriage, I still struggle with self-image, with seeing myself the way others see me. Rob is often urging me to eat more, and more often.

My relationship with my father has grown stronger in the years since Mom died, for many practical reasons (taking on the IRS is best faced as a team) and others that are purely emotional—the bonds you form during trauma are, in my experience, the most ironclad kind.

When my mother was alive she did her best to keep us from being close. Sometimes she attributed her hurtful comments about my appearance to something Dad had told her in private. Sometimes she told him I was the one who was unhappy on the farm or in our small town. The distance she created between us was strategic in her getting away with what she did; a united front would have been a formidable thing to contend with. Ultimately, she was right: my father and I make a pretty amazing team.

These moments on the farm with my father don't happen as often now, though I make it a point to get home over Christmas break and during the summer. The next time I visit, the kittens won't be kittens anymore; they'll be lanky, languid barn cats. They'll still live with the turkeys and the donkeys and Foghorn, the mean rooster who steals their kibble. They'll still live in the same open space as their mother, though they'll no longer share her straw-bale bed or rush to her side when the outside dogs howl. Their tufts of silver fur will have long ago scattered to the winds. And in the evenings, as the sky blooms pink and red with another Indiana sunset, they'll chase one another through the tidy rows of soybeans or the tangled swatch of woods at the edge of our land. They'll be free, strong enough to wander wherever they want, as far as they wish to go.

ACKNOWLEDGMENTS

This book began as a Microsoft Word document of recollections of my child identity theft experience in 2013, shortly after identifying that my mom was the perpetrator. Its journey from a running account of my memories to a published book would not have been possible without the input and guidance of many individuals.

First, my agent, Lauren Sharp at Aevitas Creative Management was instrumental in this process. After hearing me mention that I wanted to write a book about my experience as a child identity theft victim on a podcast, she reached out to me because she saw the potential in my story. Lauren connected me with Ashley Stimpson, a fellow Midwesterner, who assisted me in telling my story in a way that the general public would want to read it. To really understand me and other characters in this story, Ashley made two trips to Indiana during the writing of this book and met many of the individuals named in the book. We also spent many hours talking on the phone about the book's content.

My editor, Gretchen Young of Grand Central Publishing, has provided careful guidance regarding the structure of the book and her assistant, Emily Rosman, has answered many questions from me about the publishing process.

The process of writing this book has taught me a lot about

the history of my family. This would not have been possible without candid conversations with my dad, John Betz; uncle, Larry Lothamer; cousin, Michele Eichman; Harriett Hutson; Greg and Kathy Beumer; Kerry Beatty; Maxine and Garrett Moore; Sandy Milton; Candice Millikan; Sonny Ware; and Steve Diener.

Several of the photos in the book were made possible by my dad, John Betz, and a former graduate student of mine, Laura Sprague.

Completing this book has been a marathon, and "crossing the finish line" with it would not have been possible without the support and encouragement I have received from colleagues in the Department of Consumer Sciences and College of Education and Human Sciences at South Dakota State University.

All photos are courtesy of the author unless otherwise noted. Pages 46, 84, 206, and 250 courtesy of John R. Betz. Pages 166 and 181 courtesy of Laura Sprague.

ABOUT THE AUTHOR

AXTON BETZ-HAMILTON has made understanding the nuances of identity theft her life's work. She has a master's degree in consumer sciences and retailing and a PhD in human development and family studies, focusing on child identity theft and elder financial exploitation perpetrated by family members. She teaches at South Dakota State University.